"Finally! Just what we were waiting for: a couple of rightwing gun nuts who married above their station ask, 'What Would Ward Cleaver Do?' The American family will never be the same."

—**JONAH GOLDBERG**, senior editor of *National Review* and nationally syndicated columnist

"Jim and Cam are, as this book shows, very funny. And their wit packs wisdom. In describing what a good father looks like, they tell readers how to be one, and why they might *want* be one. I certainly never expected Geraghty to perform a public service, and yet he has. I have to go lie down now."

—**PEGGY NOONAN**, columnist for the *Wall Street Journal* and former speechwriter for Ronald Reagan

"Tough problem. Fun reading! Geraghty and Edwards tackle rampant Peter Pan syndrome with fast-paced writing, goofy recollections, and plenty of self deprecation. Bottom line: growing up is not the end of life, folks, but the stuff of life! Suffused with gratitude for their own wives and children, the whole book is a heartfelt pep talk for young men who've gotten the message that taking the plunge means walking the plank. Come on in, the water's fine, say Geraghty and Edwards! Now, if they'd just take their own advice and move out of my basement . . ."

—**MARY KATHARINE HAM**, editor-at-large of *Hot Air*, contributing editor to *Townhall Magazine*, and Fox News contributor

"We live in a time where growing up and becoming a real man is laughed at, but the authors of *Heavy Lifting* get it; it's not our accomplishments in this life that become our defining moments, it's what we pass on to our children. Being a father means leaving a legacy, and one that goes on long after we are gone."

—**STAFF SERGEANT CLINTON ROMESHA**, U.S. Army (Ret.), Medal of Honor recipient

"Boys, it's time to man up. *Heavy Lifting* is a hilarious, sound advice book every man should have. Cam Edwards and Jim Geraghty prove that growing up and taking responsibility is not only awesome, but the best way to go through life. There comes a time to buy real clothes, learn life skills, hold your alcohol, properly date one woman at a time (and no, Tinder does not count), make serious commitments, and get a job that can turn into a career. That time is now. Don't fight the man, *be* the man, and for God's sake, get your own place!"

—**KATIE PAVLICH**, Townhall.com editor and Fox News contributor

"The thing about being a man that few will tell you, but that comes through like the *Rocky* theme in *Heavy Lifting*, is that being a real man is a hell of a good time. You get to be the man of the moment. The can-do man. The man of action. The man who knows a drink should refine a man, but never define a man. There is a lot more to it, of course, but that is why Cam Edwards and Jim Geraghty wrote this book."

—**FRANK MINITER**, author of the *New York Times* bestseller *The Ultimate Man's Survival Guide*

"If ever a man was made better by marriage and fatherhood it was Jim Geraghty. He and his coauthor Cam Edwards prove that growing up, getting a job, and starting a family aren't the beginning of your life, but really the end of it. No—wait. Other way around, right? You'll have to read the book to find out."

—**JAMES LILEKS**, author, columnist, radio personality, and blogger at lileks.com

Heavy Lifting

Heavy Lifting

Grow Up, Get a Job, Start a Family, and Other Manly Advice

JIM GERAGHTY & CAM EDWARDS

REGNERY
PUBLISHING
A Division of Salem Media Group

Regnery® is a registered trademark of Salem Communications Holding Corporation

Cataloging-in-Publication data on file with the Library of Congress

ISBN 978-1-62157-414-9

Published in the United States by
Regnery Publishing
A Division of Salem Media Group
300 New Jersey Ave NW
Washington, DC 20001
www.Regnery.com

Manufactured in the United States of America

10 9 8 7 6 5 4 3 2 1

Books are available in quantity for promotional or premium use. For information on discounts and terms, please visit our website: www.Regnery.com.

Distributed to the trade by
Perseus Distribution
250 West 57th Street
New York, NY 10107

To my sons,
You are my most important work.

—Jim Geraghty, September 8, 2015

To E., for everything.
And to my children, with all my love.

—Cam Edwards, September 8, 2015

CONTENTS

PART IV - FATHERHOOD

PART V - DADS OUT AND PROUD

Meet Your Guides to Manhood

Jim Geraghty

Raconteur, man-about-the-house, father, journalist, world traveler. You can *trust* him.

Cam Edwards

A man with his own national radio show actually named after him (*how cool is that!*). Father of five, man-about-the-farm, armchair historian, and avid gun owner—*you better trust him!*

Ward Cleaver

Remember the sort of men who could fix anything (from a lawn mower to a martini), dress for success (and achieve it), never complain, make everything look effortless, marry a perfect wife, lead a moral life, and be a great dad? That's Ward Cleaver—he's not just a man, but *the man* and our ultimate channeled authority.

PART I
Breaking Away

It takes courage to grow up and become who you really are.

—E. E. Cummings

1
Ward Cleaver Was a Stud

 Now that I have your attention—and your skeptical cackling—let me tell you why.

Inevitably, when you make the assertion that Ward Cleaver was a stud—I know this from experience—people are going to accuse you of wanting to go back to the 1950s.

And that's not quite what Cam and I are advocating. Let's skip over all of the accusations that we're archaic, stodgy curmudgeons with hopelessly outdated thinking and nostalgia masquerading as advice and ideas. If you really think we're advocating for a return to docile housewives submitting to their husbands, you need to meet Mrs. Edwards and Mrs. Geraghty.

A loud corner of American culture has been rebelling against the image of the 1950s since, oh, the 1950s, so this marks our sixth or seventh decade of national cultural insurrection against the Ozzie-and-Harriet image of American suburban bliss. It's almost as if the rebellious counterculture—which has been the mainstream culture for at least a decade or two—needs the 1950s as an opponent to define itself in opposition.

So here's the first step: Can we at least acknowledge that in the two generations of rebellion and rejection of that archetypical 1950s suburban dad image, we threw some metaphorical babies out with that bathwater? Can we recognize that for all of his flaws, if today's men emulated some of Ward Cleaver's traits, the world would be a better place?

Even if Ward Cleaver comes across as boring and buttoned-down compared to today's pop icons, he's a man who takes care of business inside and outside the home. He's responsible, a man everyone can count on. We can quibble about whether his methods of fatherhood and being a good husband are *ideal*, but it's indisputable that he loves his wife and kids and tries to take care of them. He works hard, and we don't hear him complaining. His offered wisdom and guidance to the kids might seem corny or saccharine to today's ears, but it's rarely bad advice.*

He's not rebelling against anything. He's the *man*, and he wears that title with pride.

Even if you don't remember or care to remember Ward Cleaver of the show *Leave It to Beaver*, his name is now synonymous with the image of the 1950s dads—an image also shaped by Ozzie Nelson of *The Adventures of Ozzie and Harriet*, Jim Anderson from *Father Knows Best*, and, one could argue, George Bailey in the 1946 film *It's a Wonderful Life*. They were grown-ups who had already been through a Great Depression and in many cases were veterans of World War II or, later, the Korean War.

Their archetype outlasted the 1950s—Steve Douglas of *My Three Sons*, Mike Brady of *The Brady Bunch*, Howard Cunningham in *Happy Days*, Alan Thicke's Jason Seaver in *Growing Pains*, Cliff Huxtable in *The Cosby Show*. (Let's just skip over the recent controversies of Bill Cosby.) Today's DVR offers a handful of somewhat bumbling successors like Phil Dunphy on *Modern Family* and Andre Johnson of *Black-ish*.

---

* There's more sly cynicism than our memories might suggest. From the opening narration of one show: "You know, it's only natural for parents to feel proud of their children. And there's nothing so fascinating as your own offspring. But when another parent raves about his children, it's amazing how you can lose interest."

These men all had flaws, but in the end, they were solid and dependable. The word that probably best summarizes the Ward Cleavers of the world and their successors is "responsible," and maybe they seem like such throwbacks because the rest of our culture has so thoroughly embraced irresponsibility.

Ask women what they really want to see in a man—well, women who have grown out of their adolescent fascination with bad boys—and they won't say Ward Cleaver, but they'll describe at least some of his traits: Reliable. Trustworthy. Smart. Confident, but not smug. Funny and capable of laughing at himself. Successful at work, but not a workaholic. Likes kids, but is not a kid.

It's an indisputably masculine figure. It's alpha male, but a particular brand of alpha status. It's not a Gordon Gekko "Greed Is Good" alpha male. There's not much chest-pounding; the Ward Cleavers of the world don't constantly remind people of *what* they want to be; they already *are* who they want to be.

A man who's constantly telling other people what a nice guy he is isn't really all that nice. A guy who insists he's funny isn't all that funny. And a guy who constantly feels the need to showcase his confidence in himself probably has deep-rooted, hidden anxieties. If you feel the need to flaunt something, you don't really have it.

Ward Cleaver knows it's *not* a sign of weakness to admit he's wrong, when he is, and to make amends. He considers that natural honesty and courtesy. He's respectful to those who rank above him, but isn't afraid to respectfully speak his mind.

And make no mistake, most women like, appreciate, and prefer an indisputably masculine man who takes earned, quiet pride in who he is.*

Ward Cleaver isn't flamboyant, and he wouldn't have much respect for the transformation of the word "drama." Somewhere along the line, the word "drama" stopped meaning just a type of performance and came to mean a consistent aura of controversies, disputes, spats, hurt feelings,

---

* A bit of perfect irony: back in 1999, Vice President Al Gore hired feminist commentator and author Naomi Wolf to advise him on shaking the "beta male" image.

miscommunications, rivalries, and other emotionally fraught headaches. If you know people with a lot of "drama," well, I'm sorry. They're often exhausting to be around, pulling you onto their own internal psychic hamster wheel of perpetual outrage, usually relating to their infinite capacity for indignation over someone else's lack of respect for them.

Ward Cleaver ain't got time for that. In fact, there's a remarkable *lack* of drama around a Ward Cleaver type. He can act quickly, but he's not impulsive; he makes the best decision he can with the information he has at the time and acts, and accepts the consequences.

Perhaps most important, he takes responsibility—for himself and for those who depend on him. He doesn't make excuses. He doesn't whine, fume, or brood in defeat; he knows that his hard work and persistence will eventually win the day, if not this day.

And there's a lot he's simply outgrown. He never had any interest in perpetuating his own adolescence. He's a grown-up who accepts marriage and fatherhood as the life of an adult.

Now, we're not saying that Ward Cleavers of the world are off-limits to criticism, mockery, or lampooning. We're just pointing out that there was a time not that long ago when men were expected to work hard, make a good living, be good husbands and neighbors and friends, and raise and be the role models for the next generation of young men. Sure, laugh at them, but remember they're what the world is built on. If all the slackers in the world disappeared tomorrow, the video game industry would collapse. If all the Ward Cleavers of the world disappeared tomorrow, civilization would collapse.

Deadbeat dads, slacker ManChildren "failing to launch," commitment-phobic boyfriends stringing along their girlfriends as the biological clock ticks louder and louder—Cam and I aren't going to be able to solve every problem in the world in this book.

But what we can do is tell every guy out there that "growing up"—a career, a wife, kids—is *not* a trap. Working your way to a mortgage, getting married, being a father, are probably the best things that will ever happen to you. Our culture snickers at Ward Cleaver types, but it is propagating a myth when it paints them as boring, stifled, miserable, hollowed-out men, yearning for their carefree bachelor days and regretting all their commitments. What leaves a man depressed and hollow inside is not attachments but the lack of them.

Come on: gainfully employed, married, a dad—you have no idea how great your life can be. But we're about to show you.

2

College Does Not Prepare You for the Real World

If you don't know this already, you should.

Don't get us wrong. We're all in favor of education, but college today, for many people, is really just one last (and increasingly lingering) avoidance of the real world. High school actually does a lot more to prepare you for adulthood, particularly in terms of how you'll be spending most of your day: at work.

In college, you can structure your schedule to fit your desires for the most part.* Want to have all of your classes over by noon? Don't want to take a class before noon? No problem. Hey, what about scheduling all of your class times on Tuesdays and Thursdays? Then you've got five days a week free to work, study, and drink until your liver pleads for mercy!

---

* We realize that this isn't always the case. In Cam's first semester of college, he got saddled with a journalism lab that started at 7 a.m. on a Friday morning.

High school was all about the schedule. You might have been able to pick an elective or two, but you knew where you were going to be from 7:50 a.m. until 3:35 p.m. Monday through Friday. It didn't matter if you were not a morning person, or if you thought you'd do better academically with a four-day weekend.

Just like in high school, in the real world most people don't get to pick their work schedule, nor do they get to change it up every four months. Even in the gig economy, your schedule is much more likely to depend on the needs of the person paying you than on your own wants and desires. You may tell potential employers that you only work on Tuesdays and Thursdays, but you're not likely to get a job that will allow you to live anywhere other than the bedroom you slept in as a kid.

In college, skipping class isn't really a big deal. Some professors don't take attendance, and it's rare that your instructor (who's more likely to be an overworked teaching assistant than a professor) is going to give you a hard time when you show up for your next class. In many classrooms, you're expected to know the material when it comes time to take the test, but attendance isn't mandatory.

Professor Kelli Marshall doesn't have a mandatory attendance policy in her media and film courses at DePaul University, and she told *USA Today* in 2012 that while it's not completely sure she's doing the right thing, she "would hope it is since it suggests I'm treating them as adults."[*] Actually, she's not treating them as adults; she's treating them like irresponsible college students.

In high school, skipping class is a pretty big deal. Between the two authors, not a single class was skipped in our high school years (at least as long as you don't count Senior Skip Day). The closest either of us ever got to truly skipping school was the day Cam tried to go off campus for lunch and got busted.

---

[*] Rachel Osman, "Should Class Attendance Be Mandatory? Students, Professors Say No," *USA Today*, March 25, 2012, http://college.usatoday.com/2012/03/25/should-class-attendance-be-mandatory-students-professors-say-no/.

In the real world, skipping out on work usually doesn't end well either. We don't know of any job where attendance isn't mandatory.

We're pretty sure that even professors at DePaul have to turn up to teach their classes—one of the few ways academia resembles the real world, though we imagine it won't be long before professors are protesting that attendance should be voluntary for faculty as well as students.

The reason so many college students party to excess is because they can—their schedules allow it, and they have few responsibilities and no parents to ground them. In high school, your social life revolves around the hours between the time school lets out on Friday afternoon and whenever your curfew is on Saturday night. Sunday is probably homework day, and then you're back to the grind early Monday morning.

Once again, when you're out of college your social life looks a lot more like your experience in high school. With the exception of a happy hour or two, you're not likely to be doing much carousing when you have to get up at 6 a.m. to get ready for work.

"College was, and probably will be," Katie Brennan wrote at the website thoughtcatalog.com, "the only time in our lives we were truly a part of something greater than ourselves; a rare and wonderful time we were a part of a true community. A community in which we did everything together at a place we all learned to love and call home."

That actually describes high school better than college. You don't do "everything together" on a college campus, except perhaps the mandatory sensitivity training. And more important, when it comes to being "part of something greater than ourselves…a place we all learned to love and call home," getting married and having kids is a lot more real and profound version of that than going to Vassar or Party U.

Brennan muses that "While college didn't prepare me for soul-crushing Excel spreadsheets…, it taught me the most important lesson: People can be crappy to one another, but when it comes right down to it, we are all basically good."

If that's the most important thing she learned in four or five years of college, she wasted a lot of money. Maybe she should spend more time on her Excel spreadsheets. The average college graduate of the class of 2015 owes about $35,000 in student loan debt, and with interest rates between 4 and 7 percent, that's more than $300 a month in student loan payments.* That's a lot of money to spend to learn that people are basically good except when they're not. You don't need a college classroom to teach you about human nature.

High school, on the other hand, imposes no student debt while teaching a lot about human nature for anyone with their eyes open. It's true that many high school students these days can't put the Civil War in the right century or even name the founders of our country, but they should leave high school knowing the importance of showing up, doing your work, and enjoying your free time when you can.

College isn't always a mistake—but the dirty little secret is that for a lot of people it is; it comes down to stacking up lots of debt and putting off responsibility, while not learning much at all. There are obvious exceptions, especially if you've graduated with a degree in science, technology, engineering, or mathematics. But let's stop pretending that the "college experience" is a necessary or beneficial one for everybody. It isn't.

What Would Ward Cleaver Do?

He went to college, but he did it the old-fashioned way, studying a real academic discipline (philosophy), belonging to a fraternity, and dating the woman who would soon be his wife—and then getting on with the business of being an adult.

---

* Jeffrey Sparshott, "Congratulations, Class of 2015. You're the Most Indebted Ever (For Now)," *Wall Street Journal*, May 8, 2015, http://blogs.wsj.com/economics/2015/05/08/congratulations-class-of-2015-youre-the-most-indebted-ever-for-now/.

3
Getting Your Own Place

 Dear God, you've got to get out of your parents' house.

Yes, I know it's easier than finding and paying for your own place. Yes, in many places, the rent seems too darn high.

Yes, living at home with Mom and Dad can often include perks like laundry service and the freedom to raid the fridge and a cable package you probably couldn't afford if you were living on your own.

But you've got to get out of there. I want you to imagine my voice as one of the supporting characters calling the protagonist in a horror movie, informing him that the condemned old chainsaw factory that they're wandering around was built upon a Native American graveyard, then used by the government for secret bioweapon mind control experiments before a UFO crashed into it and made it the nesting ground for cursed gypsy werewolves. *You've got to get out of there, do you hear me? Get out of there now!*

Living at home, in the same circumstances you did as a teenager, inhibits growth, even under the best of circumstances and with parents with the best of intentions.

Behold the one critical tale of my parents I'm willing to share publicly:

After freshman year, I needed a summer job, and got one working the late shift in a warehouse for Baxter Healthcare Supply. My job was to stock shipping pallets from 4 p.m. to whenever the work was done, which was midnight on a good night and 4 a.m. on the much more frequent bad nights. The rest of the staff was *not* college kids working for a few months. Sweaty, grunt-inducing warehouse work wasn't a summer job to these guys; this was their job, and you can probably imagine the warm welcome they gave the college kid. (In their defense, "insufferably smug" came pretty naturally to me then…and some would probably say I never lost it.) But the upside was that I was working fifty-five to sixty hours a week, and making lots of overtime money. I calculated that in about eight weeks, I'd have all the spending money I needed for the coming year in college, and plenty extra for the rest of the summer, too.

As you can probably imagine, working the night shift is hellacious for your body clock. I remember trying, and failing, to fall asleep as the sun came up and my room got brighter and brighter even with the shades drawn. It was a brutal schedule: clock in at 4 p.m. Monday, work until 3 a.m. or so Tuesday, come home and collapse in bed, sleep until early afternoon, eat, go back, and do it again for another four days. The weekends were my lone respite.

At the end of each night/morning, I'd dump my clothes on the floor. Finally, after a few weekends, my parents observed the obvious: if my room looked like any more of a disaster area, it would qualify for FEMA relief funds. My parents told me I wouldn't be allowed to go out Saturday night if my room wasn't cleaned. Brimming with the unearned confidence that comes from living for an entire eight months away from home, I refused. They told me I was grounded.

My contention that I was too old to be grounded was probably deeply undermined by my response, which was the most spectacularly childish tantrum you've ever seen from an eighteen-year-old. Yelling, screaming, stomping, pounding the walls with my fists. I am embarrassed just writing this. Later I made the more mature observation that had there been a military draft, my parents would have told the Pentagon that I couldn't go because my eighteen-year-old butt was grounded.

It's hard for parents to accept that their child, even if over eighteen, is a grown adult, capable of making his or her own decisions. Don't blame them; they can remember the day they brought you home from the hospital like it was yesterday—and some part of them is always going to perceive a sense of supreme vulnerability around you that cannot be explained rationally. No matter how big you get, you are their baby.

My parents expected that their child would have a clean room (although I seem to recall this rule getting less strictly enforced for my younger brother). I expected that as I had been living away at college for a year, and was working long hours now, that I was entitled to leniency from such rules.

That was the last summer I lived at home. I love my parents, but I greatly prefer living under my own roof, setting my own rules.*

Don't Kid Yourself, Your Parents Want You to Grow Up

The freedom and responsibility of making your own rules under your own roof—or even negotiating the rules with a roommate(s) or housemates is an increasingly rare one for young men. The Census Bureau calculated in 2012 that 59 percent of guys ages eighteen to twenty-four and 19 percent of twenty-five- to thirty-four-year-olds live at home.**

The good news is that steep drop from twenty-four to twenty-five. The bad news is the length of that latter period, meaning some significant

---

* This is not to say that the conscious or subconscious battles over household supremacy will end in later adulthood. When you get your own place, and your parents visit, you will find that little objects—potholders, corkscrews, spatulas, etc.—tend to get put back where your parents think the objects should go, not where you keep them.

** Sandy Hingston, "The Sorry Lives and Confusing Times of Today's Young Men," *Philadelphia*, February 20, 2012, http://www.phillymag.com/articles/the-sorry-lives-and-confusing-times-of-today-s-young-men/#bihq9fHB4JivFVU1.99.

portion of grown men in their early thirties are still saying "goodnight, mom" before bed.

What's fascinating is that some of these guys are convinced that this arrangement is good for them and good for their parents, as a *Philadelphia* magazine interview depicts:

> Now, life with his parents is wearing on him. "If you want to watch TV, there's just the den," he says. "And they're in there." I ask whether he thinks his parents might have imagined themselves doing something at this point in their lives other than sharing their home with him. "They're not really doing anything," he says, sounding a little surprised. "They enjoy me being there."
>
> James is 31. He always figured he'd be married at 31. He certainly thought he'd have a place of his own. He doesn't have a plan for the future: "Plans change, and the plan has to change really quick."*

Don't be so certain that your folks are enjoying you sitting in the den with them every night, James. Most parents are quick to say to their children that they're always welcome, and that they would never turn their kids away. But most parents also want to see their adult children thriving, successful, happy—and that includes some elements of independence, financial and psychological. A big part of being a parent is teaching a child to become an adult capable of taking care of himself— and, someday, raising his own children. A guy who has to be dragged, kicking and screaming, into a life that no longer resembles adolescence is announcing to the world that his parents didn't do something right.

When should a young man get out of the house? As soon as he can— and it's okay if he stumbles a bit on that road away from home. Yes, by leaving the nest he's facing all kinds of risks and things that could go

---

* Ibid.

wrong: a bad roommate experience, a bad housemate experience, insufficient hot water, clogged toilets and drains, the need to fumigate, a broken air conditioning unit in the middle of summer, and so on. But leaving the nest is necessary to create your own nest.

(Separately, there is nothing quite like the feeling of confronting one of those minor household crises and managing to fix it by yourself.)

A guy who puts off leaving his parents' house is putting off the rest of his life, and trying to dodge a date with destiny.

We hope your parents are wonderful. They are irreplaceable. They are your safety net. They will always love you and always forgive you. But they are also not representative of life.

Landlords, with their immovable deadlines, skeptical glares, and unforgiving demeanor are much more representative of what the "real world" holds. And eventually, everyone needs to learn how to deal with the real world.

What Would Ward Cleaver Do?

Ward Cleaver was a Seabee in World War II and got married not long after college to his high school sweetheart. He knew how to take care of himself. He didn't stay at home, he made a home.

▪|||▪ MAN TIPS ▪|||▪

Don't Buy a "Tiny House"

Don't be tempted by fashionable "tiny houses" just so you can say you're a "homeowner." In case you haven't heard of them, "tiny houses" are portable tiny homes you can tow around (or plonk down on a tiny patch of land to live in tiny style).

NPR had a segment in 2015 on tiny houses in the course of which the host of the show, Tom Ashbrook, interviewed a caller from Nashville named Kevin.* He was a recent college grad and a freelance cellist and loved the idea of a "tiny house."

"I just love how perfect it is for my age and for enterprising young people that don't want to get lost in that culture..."

"When you say 'that culture,'" Ashbrook interjected, "you mean sort of that McMansion suburbia?"

"I think I mean more generally when you get through college you realize I gotta get a job to make money that I'm not necessarily going to be keeping or putting towards something, I guess really investing in something that makes you happy, I guess. I mean, you get a job to go straight to a car payment, or you get a job to go straight to a house payment...."

What Kevin was saying in fact was "I have no interest in being an adult by the traditional definition of the word, and you need to respect my desire to be a ManChild." But the fact is, adulthood, unlike a tiny house, actually IS awesome. Even with car payments. Even with a mortgage. Even with unexpected bills. And you can't

---

* "Big Potential for Tiny Houses," *On Point with Tom Ashbrook*, March 4, 2015, http://onpoint.wbur.org/2015/03/04/tiny-houses-micro-apartments.

become a serious cellist/brewmaster/IT professional/professional of any kind, especially with a wife and kids, if you live in a tiny house. Tiny houses only have enough room for you and your baggage.

Tiny houses tell the world, "Stay Away!" Are you going to invite some friends over for a tiny barbeque? A cozy night of playing games? ("Steve, we're gonna need you to sit on the toilet. Sorry, but we ran out of chair space.")

Tiny houses have always been with us. They used to be called hovels or shacks. Then we figured out how to market them to people concerned about their environmental footprint. Yes, sure, tiny houses may appeal to other demographics (agoraphobics, perhaps), but many people who purchase a tiny home are looking to discard their worldly possessions and to live more simply, more honestly, without all of the trappings of our materialistic postmodern society. Most of the time they're fooling themselves—you notice they prefer a $60,000 tiny house to a $34,000 double-wide trailer or a used RV. One is way cooler than the other. So much for being post-material.

And it seems that many owners of tiny houses don't limit themselves to a couple hundred square feet. They store some of their stuff at grandma's house or build more tiny houses for teenage children or guests. When you've got multiple tiny houses, you're kind of defeating the purpose.

Don't get a tiny house. Get an apartment—or rent a real house—with some friends.

4
Living with Roommates

Living with someone is quite different from being friends with them. Cohabitation means you will be exposed to just about every little quirk and flaw they have. Snoring, bathroom habits, bathroom maintenance, shower duration, messiness vs. cleanliness, whether they leave food out, whether they allow the dust bunnies under their bed to grow in size until they belong in Jurassic Park. Cohabitation means you get exposed to all those little things they hide from the outside world. Sometimes it's easier to negotiate all of those issues with a stranger, with no emotional baggage or delicate friendship to maintain, than with a best friend.

Of course, there's always the chance that the stranger you're moving in with is an axe murderer. It's a trade-off.

 I must begin this chapter by openly declaring I was a terrible roommate. Sorry, Chris. I don't know if my

friendship with Chris grew stronger after I moved out, but it definitely ran smoother.

We were a good Oscar-and-Felix combination. He was neat and organized; I was…not. I was basically the antimatter to neat and organized.

Probably my worst trait as a roommate was that, fairly regularly, the bacteria in my dirty laundry pile would evolve into an advanced civilization. Bacterial cities, trade routes, advanced societal specialization of roles—everything you played in Sid Meier's *Civilization* was developing in my pile of sweaty shirts. The moment you could see the little bacteria developing a space program to colonize other laundry piles, it was game over.

In my defense, washing laundry in our building was an epic hassle, particularly from my current perspective of comfortable near-middle-aged suburban married life. We lived in an apartment building with several hundred people, and our only option was the washers and dryers in the basement. (I don't think there was a neighborhood laundromat.) Each washer and dryer needed, if I recall correctly, seventy-five cents, payable only in quarters. So if you were going to wash your whites and your coloreds, you had to have at least three dollars in quarters. Of course, if your loads were too big, the machine wouldn't work properly, the load would get imbalanced, and/or the detergent wouldn't reach certain parts of the laundry. Even in my twenties, I was roughly the size of a house, so my clothes were always big and my laundry piles were always gargantuan Dagwood sandwich–piles of scientifically groundbreaking stink. Yes, I let the laundry pile up until it was about one step away from being compost.

There were four washers and four dryers in our apartment building's laundry room, presuming none of them were out of order. Of course, most nights, at least one of them was. And equally predictably, most of the several hundred renters in the building had the same thought of doing laundry on Sunday nights, to be ready for the week ahead, resulting in extraordinary demand and extremely limited supply. A standard drying cycle was maybe, on a good night, enough to get your clothes to only slightly damp. Wait, it gets worse; I think they locked the door to the laundry room at midnight. At about 11:30, that last dryer was the laundry equivalent of the last helicopter out of Saigon.

Early-twenty-something Jim was really not good at coordinating (A) having at least three dollars in quarters, and probably ideally six dollars, (B) laundry detergent, (C) fabric softener, (D) a washing machine open when I needed it, and (E) a dryer open when I needed it. It was like a rare astrological planetary alignment.

So Sunday night's laundry effort—let's not call it "doing" laundry, let's call it "trying" laundry—was to prioritize the five shirts, five pants, five pair of underwear, five pair of undershirts, and ten socks that I needed for class or work. Everything else was a luxury. Did my workout clothes require a hazmat team yet? Eh, they can wait until next week. Okay, that sock has so much dried sweat in it that it looks and feels fossilized—put him in the priority pile. The armpits of that undershirt were so yellow you would think I sweated lemons. Put him in the "must-do" pile.

All the stuff that was deprioritized? "Eh, I'll wash them next Saturday!" (SPOILER ALERT: I didn't.)

You want to talk about married, suburban luxury? Today I can throw something in the washer whenever I want. I'm Henry VIII, baby.

I was late with the rent check a couple of times, and that's a thoroughly awful feeling. I'm sure Chris felt that his credit score would be irrevocably damaged by my inability to turn in a check on time. He's now a successful consultant, living in Florida, with a beautiful wife and child. But just think of where he would be if I hadn't been late with the rent check those times! He'd probably be wealthy and powerful enough to fire Donald Trump!

Your Room Should Not Be a Roach Motel

Unfortunately for my past roommates, my story is much like Jim's. Okay, I was never, to the best of my recollection, short on rent, but I was equally slobbish in my behavior and lack of cleaning habits. It was worse, of course, when I lived with someone who was almost as messy as I was.

At one time I lived in a serviceable two bedroom apartment in a not-quite-yet-gentrified neighborhood in Oklahoma City. Even with our scavenged couch, vintage 1970s floor lamps found at Goodwill, and bookshelves made from milk carton crates and 2x4s, it was a cool place.

I suppose the best roommates might be two neat freaks, but even then there might be arguments over which brand of disinfectant to use, who puts on the hazardous waste suit to take out the trash, and so on. Two slobs presents their own problems: stacks of dishes piled high out of the sink and overflowing onto the counter, the bugs that come with the filth, picking your wardrobe by smell instead of sight, and did I mention the freaking BUGS? Bugs are *not* desirable house guests.

Roaches are filthy. But if you develop a roach problem shortly after moving into several different apartments, that might mean that you're filthy too. Roaches only hang around where they can find an easy meal and a snug place to sleep at night. It takes fifteen minutes, at the most, to pick up your trash, wash your dishes, and tidy up your apartment. *Just do it.*

Fun fact: At some point my wife will read this book, including the preceding paragraphs. She is very likely to laugh derisively and then track me down wherever I might be at the moment to shove these paragraphs under my nose and confront me about the rather slobbish behavior of several of our own children. She will almost certainly tell me that this is clear evidence I am to blame for the fact that the majority of our kids would be happy living in the kind of squalor that should be highlighted on a reality show called *Junior Hoarders*. Maybe not happy, but comfortable. It wouldn't bother them enough to clean things up.

It could be I *am* to blame for this. Maybe there's a "crummy roommate" gene that's responsible for my tendency to let a pile of dirty clothes accumulate in a corner of a room for several days before I put it in the laundry basket six feet away. Perhaps I'm just hardwired to let books and baseball caps slowly accumulate on my bedside table until there's no room for anything else, including the lamp that was originally the only thing on the bedside table in the first place. It's not my fault. I was just born this way.

Deep down, though, I'm not sure that's really true. For one thing, I've actually gotten a little better over the years about picking up after myself. I've even been known to decide to dust on my own, or run a vacuum over a carpet without having dropped something on it beforehand. Maybe I appreciate a clean house in a way that I didn't when I was a kid. That would certainly explain why many of my offspring are seemingly content to live in an ever expanding pile of dirty laundry and dishes in their rooms. Maybe we all reach a point in our lives when we actually do care that our living room bears a striking resemblance to the garbage pit in *Star Wars: A New Hope*.

Now, there's no telling when that epiphany might strike you. For all I know it already has and you're positively disgusted by the thought of allowing dirty dishes to sit in a sink overnight. If so, congratulations. Also, have you ever thought about cleaning houses as a job and if so, what are your rates?

There are, of course, other important aspects of being a good roommate—like, for instance, respecting the privacy of the other people you're living with. A search on YouTube for "roommate prank" turns up around fifty-eight thousand results. That means there are at least fifty-eight thousand people out there who you really don't want as a roommate. My roommate Todd and I were best friends, and I suppose we could have pranked each other without being punched in the junk as a result, but I don't think it ever crossed either of our minds. Of course, this was pre–social media, so we didn't have the potential to share our friend's embarrassment with everyone we knew (and a lot of people we didn't).

The best thing that having a roommate can do, in terms of preparing you for cohabitation with a romantic partner, is help with learning to communicate. If you're dividing the chores or the bills, it's not always going to be easy to bring up concerns or issues that you might have, but you're eventually going to learn how to do it productively. Otherwise, you're likely to end up living with someone in quiet resentment, or having your living arrangements obliterated during an hours-long epic fight over some slight thing that pushed one of you over the edge.

Thankfully, I survived The Roommate Years with all friendships intact, and all things considered, I couldn't have had a better roommate and friend than Todd. I managed to pay my rent on time, but I also monopolized Todd's computer and his dial-up Internet connection for hours at a stretch, and he rarely complained. Mostly we got along great, though, and I have a lot of great memories of drinking a beer or two and writing another song that we were sure could be a hit. The dream of rock stardom died soon after I moved out and got married, but the friendship remained for years afterward. Here's hoping your friendships with your roommates will continue long after you're no longer living together. Don't attract roaches, don't play pranks on your roommate, and (sorry, Jim) pay your rent on time, and you'll stand a much better chance of seeing that happen.

What Would Ward Cleaver Do?

As a Navy Man (he was also in a college fraternity), Ward Cleaver knew how to stow his gear, shine his shoes, stay neat, perform his duties, and get along with a wide swath of humanity. So should you.

5

Video Games and the Grown Man

Does growing up mean that you stop playing video games? Not really. In fact, the Entertainment Software Association (a trade group for the video game industry) claims the average American gamer is thirty-one years old—and getting older. The ESA says its survey of gamers indicates that the largest cohort of gamers in the country is those thirty-six and up. The common view is that slacker Millennials do nothing but play Xbox all day long, but the reality is that you're more likely to catch Dad playing *Skyrim* or *Grand Theft Auto IV* after Billy and Sally go to bed. At least we hope it's after the kids go to bed.

According to the ESA, today's gamers are almost evenly divided between men and women. You're less likely to get the evil eye from your wife or girlfriend if she too likes slaying orcs or waging online war against n00bs in online multiplayer Assassin's Halo of Duty servers. Of course, you might find that your significant other prefers different video games than you do. If you like Walter Mittyesque escapism, you might not find it playing as Sonic the Hedgehog or Donkey Kong. But, if nothing else, the data tell us that a lot of middle-aged people are still playing console games.

 I grew up alongside video games. I was four when my dad brought home a Pong game that attached to the back of our TV set. My brother, sister, and I would play for hours—or, since I was the youngest, I mostly watched them play for hours.

A few years later my parents bought us an Atari 2600 for Christmas. I remember all the big games, from *Pole Position* to *Pitfall*, with fond memories. That console consoled me when we moved from Oklahoma to a small town in New Jersey that actually banned kids under the age of sixteen from playing arcade games. For two years, I had to make do with the console versions of *Dig Dug* and *Frogger* (behold the hardships of a suburban kid in the 1980s).

From Intellivision, Colecovision, Nintendo, and Super Nintendo to Sega Genesis, Sega Dreamcast, Nintendo 64, Xbox, and Playstation, I played them all. I played computer games too, starting with *Zork* and working my way up through *MicroLeague Baseball*, *X-Wing*, *Sim City*, *Civilization*, the original *Fallout*, and *Baldur's Gate I* and *II*. I loved video games. And yet I hardly play them at all now.

I was well into adulthood before games started losing their charm for me, and honestly it wasn't some sort of newfound maturity that caused video games to lose their luster. It was the bugginess. I had been looking forward to playing *Fallout: New Vegas* for months, but within a few hours I realized I was playing a game that wasn't ready for release. As a naturally curious guy, I began reading up on how a game this buggy was let loose on the public, and I found that this was far more common than I thought. I also learned about the business model for all of those smartphone-based games: get a small number of saps to pay out real money for imaginary items. The state of the modern gaming industry started to remind me of a carnival midway. Both seemed designed to separate you from your money as easily as possible. I started to feel like a chump for supporting the system.

That realization definitely spurred a cutback in my gaming purchases, but I was still playing. While my younger kids were playing *Minecraft*, I was playing *Skyrim*. My youngest son, James, would play his *Lego Batman* game for thirty minutes every night, and after I put him to bed I'd break out *Batman: Arkham Asylum*.

The Day I Gave Up Gaming (Mostly) was a rainy afternoon, and there wasn't much point in going outside to do chores in the downpour. Instead, I happily parked myself on the couch and picked up the Xbox controller and started up a football game. It was a college football game, and my created character, a Doug Flutie–esque five-feet, seven-inch quarterback named Mac Edwards, had earned the starting job at Tech. I was three games into the season (playing seven-minute quarters) when my wife walked into the room.

"Having fun playing with yourself?" she asked with a smirk as she breezed by with a load of laundry.

As it turns out, that was the moment my relationship with gaming changed. It wasn't the sting of her one-liner that got to me. It was the fact that it was *true*. Here it was, a Saturday afternoon, and instead of playing with my kids, or helping with the laundry, or reading a book, or any number of halfway productive things, I was playing with myself. Yes, I was absolutely destroying the secondary of every team I was facing, but really, who beyond me cared? I had a sense of accomplishment while actually accomplishing nothing. From my perspective, I had worked my way up to starter, had taken my team into the college football rankings, and had thrown some unbelievable touchdown passes over the past ninety minutes or so. But anybody looking at me would have just seen a dude on a couch. And in reality, that's all I was.

It wasn't enough for me to be annoyed at the gaming industry. I had to be annoyed with myself to make a change. I put down the controller that day. I've picked it up a few times since, but mostly to play games with my kids. Every time I sit down and fire up a game, I get this nagging feeling in the back of my mind that reminds me I could be doing so much more with my time. It's not that gaming is bad; it's just that it's rarely the most worthwhile thing to do.

When I first had my Epiphany on the Couch and dropped video games entirely for a few months, I felt pretty self-righteous and sanctimonious about it. It's not like I picketed GameStop or even removed all consoles from my home. In fact, I never really changed my opinion about my kids playing video games. It didn't bother me to see them bouncing around playing *Dance Dance Revolution* or exploring Hogwarts as a Lego minifig. I had similar experiences as a kid, after all. What I didn't have were any memories of my parents playing video games. On some level, I came to feel that gamers who were adults, especially parents, were stunted in some way. I, having had this amazing epiphany about being a dude on the couch, thought that no dad should be a dude on the couch.

Then football season started. Not on my Xbox but in real life. And I realized I really wanted to be a dude on the couch, particularly on those Saturday afternoons when I could watch college football. Suddenly, I had a bit more empathy for those grown men playing video games. Why, they've probably had a hard week at work. All they want is to relax for a few hours. Who are they hurting, anyway? Some guys golf, some guys watch football, and some guys play video games. Everything in moderation, right?

So fire up the PS8 or whatever it's up to now. Just do it when you can. Don't neglect your wife, your kids, your dog, your job, other hobbies, and the college football season. You'll soon find that real life is more rewarding than virtual life every time.

There are some aspects of gamer culture I will not pretend to understand, Cam.

First, I spend hours upon hours of my workday on a computer, writing, typing, editing, and so on. So just how much of my free time do I want to spend staring at a screen and pressing buttons?*

I'm not denying that video games can be fun. I think the last time I played a video game without my kids was at your house. And about a decade ago you introduced me to "*Civ*," which is the sort of game that you start playing at 7 p.m., get really into it, and look up and realize that it's midnight...two days later.

I admit it's easier to be a video game un-enthusiast when you're terrible at them. Every time I pick up a console, my characters seem to become intensely suicidal and run directly toward the dragon or monster or oncoming gunfire. And that's while playing the *Madden NFL* game. Don't ask me how. Somehow I managed to press X, up, triangle, and B simultaneously, which triggers the game's AI to decree the owner has decided to relocate the franchise...mid-play.

Despite the statistics Cam cites, in some corners of society there is still a stigma that a grown man playing a video game is juvenile. Maybe that's unfair or outdated, but if you're going to make the choice to keep playing video games well into your adult years, you had better be ready to dispel those perceptions.

If you've got your act together in the rest of your life—a job and career path, healthy relationships, a supportive circle of friends, a reputation for reliability and responsibility—the snickering about video games ought to subside faster.

But if you don't have those things, look out. Here's a hint: if you want to change the "perception" of something—like, say, yourself—you have to change the reality of it. In fact, "perception" means to see things accurately.

Maybe the stigma around playing video games is unfair, as there are a lot of hobbies that can drive a man off on his own, hiding out in his

---

* And if I really feel like I spend way too many waking hours typing on a computer, why did I agree to cowrite a book in my limited off-hours?

man-cave: painting, woodworking, writing, some musical practice. But with all of those hobbies, a guy ends up creating something from that solitude. Even if you're a bad painter, at the end, you've got paint on a canvas; you've created something. To reverse our president, "You built that. Somebody else didn't make that happen." Some people will appreciate and respect that.

With video games the absolute most you can "create" is a high score, right? I suppose you can invite people to tour around your amazing castle in *Minecraft* or something. But it's a common view that online diversions like Second Life are for people who don't have much of a first one.

Most video games are a virtual simulation of actually doing interesting things.

A friend introduces you to two guys. One man is an actual service member or veteran. The other holds the world record in *Call of Duty*. Which man are you more impressed by? Whose hand are you more eager to shake? Who would you rather be?

Real life experiences beat video game experiences every day of the week and twice on Sundays. For example, would you rather be a great player at Madden on the Xbox, or actually go out and play flag football with some guys? Okay, you're not going to tear an ACL playing Xbox. It's the difference between telling the story later of how "I burst up the middle, grabbed the flag, and sacked him" and "I pressed the correct buttons to sack him."

Yes, there's an issue of cost for a lot of these experiences. But let's assume for a moment that you've got a decent amount of disposable income.

Would you rather play *Formula One* or *Asphalt*, or get some buddies, go to a go-kart track, and zip around for an hour or so?

Would you rather be an excellent player of *Street Fighter* or some other fighting game, or take a karate class?

Would you rather be a great player at *Grand Theft Auto*, or actually be a successful car thief? Okay, wait, maybe this exercise doesn't work for all video games.

The point is video games, fun as they are, are simulations of actual experiences. And you shouldn't settle for just a fun, active, exciting virtual life. You're capable of more. To quote every wise mentor character in every adventure movie ever, *you're destined for so much more*. And whatever it is you're destined for, it's not going to happen with you sitting on the couch, leaning left and right with the console in your hands.

Separately, how much time do you spend playing video games? Per day? Per week? That's time you could be improving yourself by reading a book, like one of those classics you should have read but never did, or learning something—you know, like a foreign language, or about history or even politics.

Maybe more to the point, if you don't have a serious relationship, recognize that when you get one, you'll have less time for video games. If you don't have a child, recognize that when you get one, you'll have *way* less time for video games. (Once they get a bit older, you'll see video games return to your life, except you'll be watching little Lego men run around, or Dora the Explorer, or something like that.)

Again, if they really give you a sense of enjoyment that you can't get from anything else in life, go ahead and play away. But you can't stop people from judging you on how much time you commit to games. Here's a student at American University, quoted in a *New York Times* article in 2006:

> "He said he was thinking of trying to cut back to 15 hours a week," she said. "I said, 'Fifteen hours is what I spend on my internship, and I get paid $1,300 a month.' That's my litmus test now: I won't date anyone who plays video games. It means they're choosing to do something that wastes their time ·and sucks the life out of them."*

How about we try to do some scoring in real life?

---

* Tamar Lewin, "At Colleges, Women Are Leaving Men in the Dust," *New York Times*, July 9, 2006, http://www.nytimes.com/2006/07/09/education/09college.html?pagewanted=all&_r=2&.

What Would Ward Cleaver Do?

That's easy: read a newspaper, a magazine, or a book; go golfing with the guys; play basketball with his sons; tinker on projects around the house or garden; play cards with— or go out with—his wife and friends. He was a grown-up.

•|||MAN TIPS|||•

Put Your Phone Away

We may look back one day and realize that Millennials were the first cyborg generation. Yes, their parents were the first real wired generation, but the Millennials were the ones to go wireless. Younger Millennials have grown up with Wi-Fi, smartphones, and the ubiquitous availability of information at the push of a button (whether the information is in fact accurate is, of course, a bit of a crapshoot). Okay, smartphones, smartwatches, and the Google Glass might not be exactly the same thing as being half robot, but really, the only thing missing is the biotic implant. Imagine all the information that you'd lose if your smartphone died tomorrow and tell me you're not using computers to supplement your own brainpower and capacity.

Millennials aren't just the first generation to have grown up with the option of constant connectivity, many Millennials are actually constantly connected. A 2015 survey by the American Press Institute found that 51 percent of Millennials surveyed described themselves as being always or mostly online and connected. By contrast, just 10 percent of Millennials said that they were rarely or never online.* Frankly, we're surprised the number was that high.

I didn't grow up in a wireless world, but I was an early adopter when it came to getting online. By the time I was thirteen I had a personal computer in my room, complete with a dial-up modem, and with a few clicks of my mouse and a painfully long wait to connect, I was

---

* "Digital Lives of Millennials," American Press Institute, March 16, 2015, http://www.americanpressinstitute.org/publications/reports/survey-research/digital-lives-of-millennials/.

hooked into a much larger world. Okay, at the time it wasn't *that* large. In fact, the World Wide Web was pretty boring. Mostly I would hang out on a local Bulletin Board System in Oklahoma City, where I made a few online friends. Every now and then a few of us would meet up at (I'm not kidding) a laser tag place called Photon, where we would run around blasting each other in an arena filled with artificial fog and bad synth music. No, I wasn't a nerd. Why do you ask? Just because I played Photon and even went to a couple of BBS meetups that were hosted, of course, at our local science museum?

By the age of sixteen, I become online friends with a girl my age in Alabama. We quickly moved from chatting online to sending actual letters to a few quick phone calls (long distance was expensive). Eventually it culminated in a road trip to Alabama to hang out with her and her friends for a weekend.*

Six years later I met my wife online, and about seven years after that I took a job hosting an online talk show. I'm pretty pro-Internet, and would, in fact, encourage everyone to check out National Review Online and NRA News' *Cam & Co.*

But even the techies are warning about our unhealthy dependence on the Internet. In his 2010 book *You Are Not a Gadget*, author, programmer, and virtual reality pioneer Jaron Lanier warned that "anonymous blog comments, vapid video pranks, and lightweight mashups may seem trivial and harmless, but as a whole, this widespread practice of fragmentary, impersonal communication has demeaned interpersonal interaction." In 2014, philosophy professor Evan Selinger sounded the alarm in *Wired* magazine that "Today's

---

* This was actually one of the rare times I violated my mom's trust growing up. She knew that I was visiting some friends in Memphis. She just wasn't aware that I was driving my 1973 Dodge Dart another three hours east to meet a girl. Looking back, I'm reasonably sure she actually would have been okay with it, but I wasn't about to take the chance at the time.

Apps Are Turning Us into Sociopaths." Selinger worries that apps like BroApp—which sends automated "sweet" texts to your significant other so you don't have to—might seem fun or appealing, but warns that "the more we outsource, the more of ourselves we lose."

Futurist Ray Kurzweil believes that by 2029 we'll have reverse engineered the human brain. We'll then have "software algorithmic methods to simulate all of the human brain's capabilities, including our emotional intelligence."* Kurzweil believes that computing power will also have grown exponentially, so that artificial intelligence will constantly improve itself, quickly outpacing human intelligence. This is known as The Singularity.**

What happens when The Singularity occurs? Maybe we all *really* become cyborgs. Maybe computer overlords enslave the human race. Maybe the world becomes a utopian paradise. Who knows?

But the sad fact is plenty of people are *already* being controlled by their machines. We all know at least one person like this, right? They're the ones who can't have a conversation without breaking eye contact every five seconds to check their phone, look at Twitter, or continue a political argument with a stranger online. Working in the media, I know a *lot* of people like this; it's encouraged. We think we need to be engaged online all the time. But I also know, from experience, that it's better to put the phone away for extended periods, to work, walk, and play outside, to be fully focused on the person in front of you, to be part of a real community. You can say it's a 24/7 news cycle and you have to practice "brand engagement" by constantly tweeting and posting, but you don't; not really. No one needs you 24/7, except your family—and they deserve your full attention.

---

* Ray Kurzweil, "The Coming Singularity," YouTube, https://www.youtube.com/watch?v=1uIzS1uCOcE.
** Ray Kurzweil & The Singularity would be a great name for a band.

PART II
Life Skills 101

Showing up is eighty percent of life.

—Woody Allen

6

The Art of Drinking

Alcohol, you probably don't need to be reminded, is dangerous. But having tried prohibition once, we're unlikely to do it again. Instead, maybe we need to focus our attention on teaching people how to drink.

Part of the problem is that new drinkers generally don't have *mentors*, they have *peers*. As a result, we tend to end up learning from experience, rather than acquired and inherited wisdom. Granted, it might be hard to learn from someone else's hangover (other than don't party with Zach Galifianakis), but left to our own devices we tend to make the same rookie mistakes generation after generation. Wouldn't it be great if we had a "Spirits Guide" to help us learn to drink?

When you (and when I say "you" here, I really mean "I") first start drinking, your thought process is something like this: *"I have alcohol. I want to get drunk. I have to go home, so I better get as drunk as possible as quickly as I can so I can be sober by the time I have to go home."*

Now, at some point in life, usually after college, you realize that there's a different kind of drunken experience to be had; one based not on getting as drunk as possible as quickly as possible, but on maintaining what I call the "Golden Zone of Inebriation" for as *long* as possible. The GZI is that state of being where you're happily buzzed, but still fully aware of your surroundings and yourself. Your tongue is a little looser, your wit a little quicker (and slightly more bawdy), and all is well with the world. Slip too far into sobriety and all of a sudden you're tired and you really don't feel like drinking anymore and you're just going to Uber home but thanks it was fun you guys. Slip too far into inebriation and all of a sudden your tongue is really loose but it seems to have grown really fuzzy and too large for your mouth. Plus, you're having a hard time focusing your thoughts (and your eyes), so you're just going to bellow inarticulately for a couple of minutes before you pee your pants in front of your drinking buddies, which includes the girl you want to marry but haven't had the courage to ask out yet. You'll lose the nickname "Pee Pants" in a couple of months, but she'll never look at you the same again.

Don't be a Pee Pants. Drink like a grown-up instead. Admittedly, that's easier said than done when it runs counter to the dominant drinking culture that you might have learned on a college campus or with the bad boys in high school. But you're perfectly capable of drinking without getting obliterated. I'm not talking abstinence here, though that's a perfectly acceptable choice. *No one* should be mocked for refraining from alcohol. (You might need them to drive you home.) We're simply talking about how to drink if you're drinking. How do you achieve your maximum GZI? Here are a few tips.

1. Change your mindset. You're not drinking to get completely 'faced, you're drinking to enjoy yourself. Instead of pounding down drinks all night, when you feel that warm, pleasant glow suffuse your body, finish that drink

and then have a glass of water or something nonalcoholic before having another drink. When you have that next drink, sip, don't chug. Maintain a pace that's more akin to a cross country run than a hundred-meter sprint.

2. Drop the sweet stuff. Sugar masks the alcohol flavor, which makes it more difficult for you to judge how much you've been drinking. Plus, if you're drinking birthday cake–flavored vodka, you need better taste.

3. Don't buy cheap booze. You can afford quality, if you're not thinking about quantity. You also won't need to mask your cheap booze with soda, fruit punch, etc. Enjoy drinking, not just being drunk.

4. Learn to say, "I'm good." As you drink more, and find the limits of your tolerance, you'll find your own GZI. A good drinker doesn't mind being the only sober one at the party, or cutting himself off to sober up, if that's what circumstances require.

Maybe the simplest guideline is this: don't be the most inebriated person in the room. In fact, depending on the size of the gathering, stay out of the top five. There's usually a painful lesson to be learned when you stray outside of the GZI. And unlike with exercise, the pain doesn't represent a gain.

The Perils of Sherry

I'm going to share two illustrative tales, one serious and illuminative, the other...not so much.

Once you're twenty-one—because none of us ever drank alcoholic beverages before we turned twenty-one, right?—you begin to realize just how off-key those heavy-handed "don't drink, kids" public service announcements were. I remember a classmate in my sixth grade health class asking why any adult would drink, because it was so obvious that once you started drinking, you were "throwing your life away." Well done, Carrie Nation.* The scaremongering curriculum blurred the difference between drinking and de facto self-immolation. Once a teen realizes that a Bud Lite isn't hemlock—cripes, it hardly qualifies as *beer*—how seriously do you think they'll take the warnings about drugs?

Here's what was largely missing from the drugs-and-alcohol instruction we received: one big reason people drink too much is because it *makes you feel good*. If you're in a miserable spot in life, the path to a better, happier, more fulfilling life can seem really difficult and far. The "hey, let's get drunk" path is a lot quicker and easier. But it's a temporary fix; after the drinking binge, whatever's making you miserable hasn't changed, and now you have a hangover.

I'm not an alcoholic, but there was a short span, shortly after turning twenty-one, when I was just flat out drinking too much, too often. It became too big a part of how I had fun.

I hated my job. My then-girlfriend, eventually-to-be-wife, was living abroad. I still had my friends around, but it was hard to see how my life was going anywhere. I had met the real world, and the real world was kicking my ass.

But after a few drinks, man oh man, everything changed! Not only was I no longer worried about people thinking I was a loser or socially awkward, but everything was hilarious! Alcohol was a social lubricant, and my life was a slip-and-slide. If you trip and pratfall while sober, you're embarrassed. If you trip and pratfall while drunk, not only do you not feel much pain, you're laughing hysterically at yourself and not the least bit worried about other people laughing at you. In that window of tipsiness, you're the guy you want to be—so cool, so at ease, so relaxed, nothing bothers you.

And so you drink—starting on Fridays and Saturdays, and maybe you drink quite a bit on Sunday watching football, too. You have something with dinner...each night of the week. When your roommate is

---

* Carrie Nation was a member of the Prohibitionist movement who used to run into saloons and attack patrons and break barrels with a hatchet. Because drunks were a danger to others, you know.

traveling, you realize you can drink as much as you like without him saying something about whether you've had enough. You count the number of sick days you have, and wonder if you can call in sick this week, free to drink as much as you like one weeknight. This was back when liquor stores were closed on Sundays in Washington, D.C., so I remember *sprinting* to the one in my neighborhood on a Saturday evening, desperate to restock before it closed for the evening.

My dissatisfaction with everything else in life prompted me to join a comedy improv troupe—cue everyone's "man, you really were drinking heavily then" comment. After my girlfriend returned from her study abroad, she saw one of our performances, and then we went out after the show to celebrate.

My idea of celebrating? Three Long Island Iced Teas in rapid succession.

Do you know what's in a Long Island Iced Tea? Vodka, gin, tequila, rum, triple sec, sour mix, and a splash of cola. At least, that's what they say is in it. Basically the bartender just starts looking for bottles under the bar that he hasn't used in a while and starts dumping them into a tall glass of ice. Because when you order a Long Island Iced Tea, you're basically telling the bartender, "I want the shortest path to utter, blotto inebriation you have. If you've got Absinthe, throw that in there, too. Vanilla extract? Sure. Rum raisin ice cream? Hey, it's got 'rum' in the name, give it a shot. Speaking of which, throw in some shots. What's that over there, lighter fluid? Hey, you only live once!"

A Long Island Iced Tea is the Price Club of drinks—lots of variety all in one place, in a portion large enough to take care of your family for a month. By the time the waitress brings a Long Island Iced Tea to your table, the garnishing lemon has already checked itself in to a twelve-step program.

Anyway, my girlfriend was not impressed with my shift from a high blood-alcohol content to a high alcohol-blood content. She didn't have to say much. She later said she thought I was trying to impress her with my ability to drink a midsized distillery's worth in one sitting. It was worse; I didn't think I was drinking that much more than usual.

I don't know if I would say I had a "moment of clarity." But I'm certain that I sure as hell didn't want her, or any of my friends, thinking of me as an alcoholic. I knew I had been drinking a lot; I just hadn't thought of it as being "too much." What's the difference between a guy who likes to drink and a guy who has a problem? I concluded the answer was control—and I set out to prove to my girlfriend, my friends, and ultimately to myself that I had that control.

I went cold turkey for six months. No alcoholic drinks, period. Afterward, I felt pretty confident that I didn't have a drinking problem or addiction.

Once I decided it was safe to drink again, I decided to try to find drinks I could nurse throughout an evening. Having renounced Long Island Iced Teas and the sweet, gulp-able screwdrivers—hey, it's got orange juice! It's practically a health drink!—I started trying out the bourbons, whiskeys, scotch, and Manhattans. Sure, they were bitter and strong—and because of that, you had to sip them and take your time. No one could tell you were nursing a drink for the entire evening with one of those.

I must warn you that ordering harder drinks like bourbon does have side effects; you can end up really liking them.

Almost every man has his worst-night-of-drinking-ever story. I'll skip to the punchline of mine—apparently yelling, "I can't find the steering wheel," in my bed after a good friend ensured my butt got home safe from a friend's bachelor party and just warn all of you, "Don't mix rum, Jack Daniels, and gin when you're dehydrated in extremely humid weather." Sorry about the plants in your backyard, Paco.

My other cautionary tale is to warn you to beware of that drink that you're not as familiar with as your usuals. The only time I've gotten sickly drunk in the past fifteen years or so came when the Mrs. and I hosted a party. The guest list was mostly her work friends, and I had visions of an awkward evening, full of boring shop talk. I warned my wife that I didn't want the workmates and spouses to split off into two groups, leaving the bunch of us groping for conversation.

My wife was cooking with sherry, and I poured myself a serving before the guests arrived. Has there ever been a less menacing sounding drink than "sherry"? Sherry! It sounds like a sweet girl who works a few cubicles down. Sherry's not going to do you wrong. Sherry's not going to sneak up on you when you least expect it!

Uh-uh. Sherry's a bad girl. Sure, she looks sweet. I'll skip the obvious joke about her going down easy. But man, when you're not looking, she'll pack a punch.

"I'm just wine!" she'll giggle playfully.

"Like hell she is!" warns your liver. "She's 15 percent alcohol by volume, minimum, maybe up to 22 percent!"

Needless to say, with "Sherry" as my constant companion at the party that evening, I was full of good cheer, although I found myself suddenly tired as it wound down. And then, once the last guest had departed...I waved a friendly farewell, closed the door...and ran to the toilet and returned all the terrific food my wife had prepared.

I learned, painfully, Sherry's not the kind of girl you can keep down for long.

What Would Ward Cleaver Do?

Drunk? Are you kidding? Ward Cleaver likes the occasional drink, but he knows how to handle it, and his drink of choice is coffee.

7

Clothes and the Man

For the most part, in high school or college no one cared how you dressed. Oh sure, you might have donned certain clothes to fit in with a particular school subculture, but for most of us it was T-shirts and jeans. You were lucky if your school had uniforms, because the fact is, if you went to West Point you're better prepared for the expectations of the real world than if you went to Slobovian U. The real world expects you to dress like the professional you claim to be.

Dressing for Success (at Goodwill)

A book called *Dress for Success* was on a bookshelf at almost every friend's house when I was kid. I didn't read it then because "dressing for success" at my age wasn't really up to me. I wore the clothes my parents bought for me. And I didn't read it later because by the time I landed my first job its ideas were firmly ensconced in the corporate world. The principle message was dress well so that business executives take you seriously.

John T. Malloy first published *Dress for Success* in 1975 when leisure suits were a thing. Can you imagine wearing a leisure suit unironically? It actually happened. Millennial men might have to deal with meggings and skinny suits, but at least they've never been told that it was desirable to look like Cousin Eddie from *National Lampoon's Vacation*. The 1970s were the nadir of American fashion. No one was spared the horror, including one little boy with a bowl haircut who was forced to wear plaid overalls with an olive green turtleneck for a cheap Sears studio photograph that would taunt him throughout the rest of his childhood from its position atop the living room mantelpiece. But I digress.

Malloy's book came out at a culturally appropriate time, and it's continued to resonate in certain sectors of the corporate world. It's undeniable, however, that clothing standards overall have become a lot more casual.

When, for example, did wearing pajamas outside become a thing? Back in 2012, a Louisiana lawmaker actually floated the idea of banning the wearing of sleepwear outside the home after seeing one too many pairs of PJs in public. Caddo Parish District Commissioner Michael Williams warned, "Today it's pajamas. Tomorrow it's underwear. Where does it stop?"

I feel for the commissioner. I really do. But the forces of the onesies are sneaky. The company Betabrand, for instance, offers "The Suitsy"— a one-piece zip-up set of pajamas that can be worn (theoretically, anyway) as a suit in an office. Actually, the Suitsy isn't billed as pajamas at all, but that's what it is. You might be able to get away with charging $380 for a zip-up suit, but there's no way you can get away with charging that much money for a pair of pajamas.

I get the comfort factor. Pajamas are super comfortable. But it's also lazy. When you leave the house in pajamas, what you are telling the world is "I'm too lazy to actually put on clothes." If clothes make the man, then wearing zip-up pajamas with feet makes the ManChild.

Now, having said that, good luck figuring out your corporate dress code. It's been pretty simple for me, but the rules are changing. For all I know you could be *required* to wear a Suitsy before long. When I was a reporter, I used to envy the television videographers because they could wear shorts and golf shirts in the Oklahoma summers. Sports reporters could get away with that dress code as well, but news reporters, even those of us who worked in radio and weren't on camera (unless we accidentally wandered into someone's live shot), were expected to look "professional." Twenty years later and I've hosted television news shows in a T-shirt and ball cap. Suits are not my thing. I'm much more likely to be found in a sport coat with jeans, and I'm never without my ballcap. But even I have standards: I don't think I'll ever host a show in my pajamas. While Jim's been known to blog in his, I think he'll probably stick to a real jacket and tie when appearing on cable news, though he might already have ordered his own Suitsy by the time you read this. No matter how casual the dress is in your work environment, you're never going to impress the people who matter by pattering around the office in your PJs.

One final point about looking professional in an increasingly casual world: not everything in your closet needs to come from a high-end brand or has to be bought at a high-end store. It's relatively easy to look professional even on a tight budget. In my mid-twenties, I would unashamedly shop for clothes at the local Goodwill. I always found something, whether it was a sport coat, some casual dress shirts, or a pair of serviceable khakis. I was able to wear better quality clothes than I could afford to buy new. And by then I had a wife to make sure I didn't accidentally buy a Cousin Eddie leisure suit or plaid overalls—one of the innumerable ways a wife can improve your life.

What to Expect When You're Not Dressing for Success

I'd just like to note that this "Dressing for Success" chapter was Cam's idea, because I can hear the scoffing about my wardrobe from here.

I walk into my closet a lot of mornings and think, *okay, what can I get away with wearing today?* What stains are least visible? You see, I have an eating disorder; too much food that I attempt to eat doesn't end up in my mouth.

It is an unfortunate fact of human physiology that anything that misses your mouth in the process of eating or drinking is destined to land, front and center, upon your shirts or ties—exactly where everyone looks at you. If, by some miracle, it misses the shirt or tie, it's going to land in your crotch, which is even worse.

My food is the Professor Moriarty to Billy Mays's and OxiClean's Sherlock Holmes—a creative, nefarious, relentlessly determined arch-nemesis, constantly driven to outdo past performances. *"Oh, you say your detergent can get rid of any stain? Challenge accepted, old bean. The game is afoot."*

You would think my lower lip had an escape hatch. If the falling nacho salsa, soup, coffee, marinara sauce,* cheese sauce, gravy, or other stain-in-waiting could just somehow adopt a magic-bullet-style trajectory, and curve around the front of me, and land on, say, my shirttail in the back, where it's obscured by the lower part of the suit jacket, my life would be so much better. Is there any way to get lobster bibs to be acceptable for all meals? Or maybe entire raincoats? I try not to be messy, but somehow I go to a neighborhood barbeque and it looks like I sat in the front row of a Gallagher performance.

I have now reached the point where if I'm going to be in front of people and need to look professional, I simply don't eat once I'm in my suit. Too many variables—the stain, the bit of spinach stuck in the teeth,

---

* I used to have a fancy watch that worked fine for a long time, then started running slow. I found a watch repairman, who opened it up and took a look. He came back and asked, "Do you eat a lot of marinara sauce?"

the irrepressible untimely belch mid-sentence. If it's a morning meeting, I'll drink coffee very carefully.

I'm not saying this is a perfect solution; I've found my stomach registering its objection to this arrangement mid-interview with Marco Rubio, and desperately hoping the microphone on my lapel didn't pick up the gurgling in my midsection. Billy Crystal's old *Saturday Night Live* character "Fernando" kept telling people, "It is better to look good than to feel good," reportedly quoting actor Fernando Lamas. This is probably a terrible philosophy for your overall life, but not a bad idea for those big meetings or moments when you absolutely need to look your best.

I work in Washington, D.C., which is allegedly a spectacularly fashion-conservative town. I don't mind that. It simplifies things. "Fifty Shades of Grey" originally referred to the acceptable palette for suits here. You know how cheesy sci-fi films usually featured a dystopian future where everyone dresses the same? For a lot of people working in the corridors of power in the nation's capital, that future is now.

Look, after hours, wear whatever the heck you want. But for every job interview, wear a suit. Unless you've been specifically directed otherwise, overdress. If you arrive at a work event dressed too formally, it's easy to adjust—loosen or remove the tie, take off the jacket, etc. It's almost impossible to overcome dressing too casually.

What's the worst that could happen, you ask?

Pity poor Lance Futch of Vivint Solar, who was invited to an event at a Utah Air Force base about helping veterans transition to the private sector.* Futch, dressed in a company polo shirt, arrived and was escorted to a small room, where he learned the event was a small, intimate meeting and that the guests included Senator Orrin Hatch and President Obama, all covered by cameras of the national press corps. But give Futch credit: his company polo shirt was stain-free!

---

* Geoff Earle, "Guy in Polo Shirt Stunned When 'Official' at Meeting Is Obama," *New York Post*, April 8, 2015, http://nypost.com/2015/04/08/man-stunned-when-meeting-with-federal-official-turns-out-to-be-obama/.

Sure, there are workplaces where dressing formally is frowned upon. Silicon Valley billionaire investor Peter Thiel says that when PayPal was starting up, they automatically dismissed anyone who arrived for a job interview in a suit, and said that he and his investors "never invest in a CEO that wears a suit." You can love this philosophy or hate it, but Thiel is enforcing Silicon Valley's own dress code: "I'm too much of a genius technology guru, contemplating the next world-changing innovation, to fuss with neckties."

Fairly or not, appearances matter. Yes, it would be a better world if everyone would assess you on your mind, your talents, your ideas, and everything that can't come across in a first visual impression. But they don't, and you can react to this hard fact in two ways. You can whine about it and make an ultimately pointless gesture of defiance by not looking your best, or you can cinch up a tie, give it your best shot, and see if it helps.

I'm on television pretty regularly, and here's a little secret: everybody focuses on the waist up. We're behind a news desk. One of cable news' biggest hosts, whose name I won't mention—okay, his name rhymes with Schmawn Schmannity—does the show in jeans and sneakers, as well as a suit and tie on top. He can pull it off; it's his show. But I wouldn't dare. Because you know that would be the night where the desk suddenly collapsed and they needed us to appear standing up. Or Schmawn Schmannity might tell me to get up from behind the desk and run a post pattern on that football he throws around as he's heading to commercial.

I have since been advised by my friend Mickey White, who worked in television a long while, that white shirts are a no-no on television; apparently they're too reflective. Blue is a nice, soft color. Patterns can be dangerous; the wrong kind of parallel lines can create a distortion effect on the broadcast.

You may say, "Eh, this doesn't matter, I don't work on television." But you work in a world where just about everyone has a video camera in their phone. Yes, not only do appearances matter, but on any given day, you can end up in some recording that could end up being seriously consequential.

What Would Ward Cleaver Do?

It's easy to imagine Ward mowing the lawn while wearing a collared shirt, maybe even a tie. He saves his gym clothes for the gym, his pajamas for bed, and while he might dress *differently* at home than he does at work, he doesn't dress less well. Dressing well is dressing courteously.

8

The Job Hunt

ooking for a job has almost always been tough.

It's been a long time since high school or college graduates could walk down to the widget factory and sign up for their forty-years-and-pension-guaranteed jobs.

Some who did that paid for their affluence and security by first living through a Great Depression or fighting in a war. The 1950s and 1960s were mostly boom times, but the 1970s were mired in stagflation and economic malaise. The 1980s saw a roaring economic recovery, but the 1990s were a boom or bust depending on your industry: dot-com (boom), aerospace and defense after the Cold War (bust). And remember all those Generation Xers then allegedly mired in McJobs? The twenty-first century has been dominated by a war on terror that few of us have had to fight (and whose soldiers, sailors, airmen, and Marines are now getting pink slips with defense cuts) and a Great Recession that wiped out a lot of jobs. Many companies have reevaluated whether they really need those entry-level, recent-college-grad positions. For you, they might have been the first rung on a career ladder. For them, they're something that an unpaid intern could do.

You can't choose the job market or economic circumstances you're in. You can only choose how you respond to that challenge.

The two keys are momentum and hunger. NFL-player-turned-motivational-speaker Eric Thomas summarized it simply, "When you want to succeed as badly as you wanna breathe, then you will be successful."

Yes, it's not fair that you're not working during a 1980s boom or a 1990s dot-com mania. But you might as well purge the words "it's not fair" from your vocabulary. For starters, every time you say it, you sound like Luke Skywalker whining, *"But I was going to the Tosche Station to pick up some power converters!"*

Yes, it's not fair that they're not handing out on street corners six-figure managerial jobs requiring no experience. Yes, it's not fair that so many companies feel so little loyalty to their employees, and that you can do your job well and still get laid off if the company hits the skids. Nobody ever said the world was fair.

And what's more, the odds are good that a lot of people around the world would say you've got some unfair advantages of your own. You might have parents that love you. You might have been raised in a safe environment. You might have gone to good schools, or at least okay ones. You might have good health. You live in a country where you're free to pursue any career you like; no authoritarian regime is dictating what you'll do with your life. There are people around the globe who don't have any of that.

("Check your privilege" is an insufferable term of derision heard on campus and in Internet debates. "Count your blessings" is the better way of putting it.)

The late sportscaster Stuart Scott, discussing his diagnosis of cancer in his memoir *Every Day I Fight*, observed:

> I haven't allowed myself a single *Why me?* moment. Because,
> if I start asking *Why me?* as it relates to cancer, I'd have to

start asking *Why me?* as it relates to all of my good fortune: Why was I able to do this job I love? Why was I blessed with [daughters] Sydni and Taelor and such a great family? Once you start questioning the bad stuff that comes your way, you have to start questioning the good—and I wouldn't trade the good for anything.*

There are choices you can make to create your own advantages. You can make the choice, for instance, to be more determined than anyone else out there.

It does seem that a lot of people swim in waters of either ignorance or misinformation about what it takes to build a successful career.

Movin' on Up

Someone once told Cam how lucky he was to have a career hosting his own radio and television shows; he didn't know, of course, about how Cam had gotten there—doing years of low-paid drudge work as an informal apprenticeship.

Cam handled that guy a lot more calmly and politely than I would have. You want to be where I am, pal? Go work sixty hours a week when Congress is in session on a complicated Rube-Goldberg-designed computer system, recording every vote of every one of the 435 members of the House, knowing that you've already been warned that if you screw up one more time you're fired. (That job was the one time in my life I've ever experienced hallucinations, because I was so overwhelmed with stress that I began remembering making mistakes that I hadn't actually made.) Then go work at some dot-coms where the financial handwriting is on the wall and you see the staff getting smaller and smaller with each round of layoffs. Then work at a wire service where the paychecks

---

* Stuart Scott with Larry Platt, *Every Day I Fight* (New York: Blue Rider Press, 2015), 25.

bounce, your competitors are making twice what you make, your computers are several years out of date, and you are your own tech support.

Even in those difficult jobs, I was making connections, building up a thick stack of clips, and demonstrating that I could do what I wanted to do: *write*. After a while, my freelance submissions stopped being from Jim Geraghty, Some Schmo, and instead were from Jim Geraghty of States News Service, whose work appears in the *Boston Globe, Bergen Record, Washington Post,* and elsewhere. I took a giant step forward when I stopped seeing my job as a burden or a source of grief and aggravation and started seeing it as a giant opportunity that few other people get. It took three years, but it finally opened the door to the dream job at *National Review.*

It's often said that one of the problems with Millennials is that they're not getting ahead because they're focused on glamour jobs that few of them will ever attain. If you want to be a professional athlete, Hollywood star, or rock star, God bless ya; I wish you the best of luck and success. When it comes to your talents in those astronomically competitive fields, your family, friends, and loved ones are probably like that poster from *The X-Files*: they *want* to believe.

Sharp minds will notice that *wanting* to believe is not the same as *believing.* You might be great at your dream profession. You might be merely okay at it. In those extremely competitive fields, there's this nagging fear that being talented might not be enough. Connections matter. Luck matters. And having something to fall back on matters (you know, working on additional skills applicable to other careers).

Relentless determination, a stubborn refusal to quit, working hard to succeed, and developing options in case option one doesn't work are crucial to your eventual success, wherever it may lie. Everyone who cares about you needs to know that whether or not you ever get that big audition or tryout, you're inevitably going to achieve *something*, and that something will help you keep a roof over your head, put food on the table, and build a happy future for yourself and perhaps someday a family.

Here are two similar expressions of this attitude, from two highly successful men:

"Don't quit your job after six months. Your first six months in most jobs can be really tough. You probably all have that experience, where you say, 'Oh, my goodness, what a mistake have I made, I gotta get outta here.' Live through the first six months. Put your head down. Work real hard. Remember to do your present job really well. Perform as superbly as you can, and then just soak up as much learning as you can. Always look for opportunities, for gaps in the marketplace, opportunities to create new innovations of one kind or another. Almost every successful entrepreneur I've seen did not begin by sitting down with a piece of paper and saying, 'Okay, I want to own my own company, what shall I do?' Instead they worked somewhere and they saw a need, they saw a problem that wasn't being met. They said, 'You know what, somebody ought to do something.... A-ha, I'll do something about that!'"[*]
—Mitt Romney

"I want the finer things in my life, so I hustle."
—Fiddy Cent

Those are two quotes to live by.

Learning on the Job

You might not be lucky enough (and yes, despite the need for hard work, perseverance, networking, and a good attitude, luck is still important) to land a job in a field that you love right away. My oldest daughter's first job out of college was in a hospital gift shop, which might have (mostly) paid the bills but certainly didn't offer much in terms of job satisfaction.

---

[*] "Romney—Secret to a Successful Career," YouTube, https://www.youtube.com/watch?v=-xcSSbmkYqs.

You might even find your career path taking you in a direction you never thought it would go.

Work can define who you are, but that doesn't mean that it always will. I remember telling my daughter after one particularly awful shift in the gift shop that "sometimes our job is fulfilling, and sometimes our paycheck allows us to do the things that fulfill us instead." My daughter is incredibly artistic, and during her time toiling in the gift shop, she was unleashing her creative forces through sculpture, painting, and photography. Eventually she made her way into the culinary world, which allows her to use her creativity in the workplace, even if not in the direction she originally intended. She's also going back to school and studying engineering, which would allow for her to use her creative side while also (hopefully) providing a good-paying job.

In 2012 Bentley University published a survey on Millennial attitudes toward work.* About half of the survey's respondents agreed with the statement that "Members of the Millennial generation have a different set of priorities than previous generations. What seems like Laziness is really evidence that they aren't willing to sacrifice control over their own personal fulfillment just to achieve success at a job. Today's young adults want flexibility to explore their own interests and develop their own identities, lifestyles, and skills. They grow impatient with situations that they find stifling, and they resent it when the demands of work take away from their personal lives."

In other words, they think of themselves as precious little snowflakes. I understand. Compared to my parents, I'm a precious little snowflake too.

My dad joined the Navy as a seventeen-year-old in 1944. He served in the Pacific in the waning days of the war on a destroyer and saw some action, mostly during the Okinawa campaign. In comparison, when I was seventeen, I thought I was a badass because I went to a writing camp at Rhodes College in Memphis, Tennessee. My mom didn't live in a home

---

* Center for Women and Business, *Millennials in the Workplace* (Waltham, MA: Bentley University, 2012), https://www.bentley.edu/centers/sites/www. bentley.edu.centers/files/centers/cwb/millennials-report.pdf.

with running water, indoor plumbing, and electricity until she was eighteen. I didn't live in a house with cable until I was seven.

That, in a nutshell, is the difference between the Greatest Generation and their progeny. And it has only gotten worse in succeeding generations, each more spoiled and coddled than the last. No matter how many trophies we get as a kid just for showing up, most of us eventually come to the realization that fulfillment comes through hard work and responsibility. You have to earn it.

My first real job on my career path was as an associate producer. I worked, as the low man on the totem pole, the graveyard shift from 11 p.m. to 8 or 9 a.m. Most of that time was spent in a draining, mad scramble working with a skeleton crew to get ready for the three-hour behemoth morning show. Scripts had to be written, printed, and distributed; last-minute changes had to be reloaded into the teleprompter, with new copies of the script run out to the anchors during commercial breaks. It was hectic and frantic, and it would have been a lot more fun if it had been done from 9 a.m. to 5 p.m.

I never got used to the graveyard shift. Every morning I would drive back to my apartment, draw the curtains in my bedroom, and immediately fall asleep. I'd wake up around 4 or 5 p.m. still feeling exhausted. I'd stumble to the kitchen and pour myself a bowl of Cocoa Krispies, and then when my roommate/bandmate/best friend Todd got home from his day job (an actual day job), we'd head over to our friend Jonathan's house to rehearse for a few hours. From there I'd head into work and do it all over again.

It was tiring, but there was a light at the end of the tunnel. Burnout was high among the associate producers, and turnover was pretty frequent. As long as I worked hard and showed progress in my ability to quickly turn a script or run the Chyron character generator, sooner or later I'd get promoted to a day shift and would finally be released from my nocturnal work schedule.

In addition to a work ethic, I was also lucky enough to have a mentor. I've been blessed to find mentors at virtually every job I've had in radio and television. Without their experience, guidance, friendship, and wisdom, I'd likely be flipping burgers somewhere. I never consciously sought a mentor, but I was always eager to learn from veterans willing to teach me.

Officially, Lisa was an assistant producer, like I was, but in reality she was producer-without-portfolio. She was in charge of all the associate producers, and could pinch-hit for virtually all of the show producers if need be. She was smart, savvy, and wickedly funny, with a blend of competence and calm that a newsroom desperately needs and so rarely gets.

As part of her duties in managing the herd of associate producers, she would note which ones of us were in over our heads, who could move onto a producer track, and who wanted a job in front of the camera. If they wanted to be on-air reporters, they'd probably soon be departing for an on-air gig in a much smaller market, where they could get experience in front of the camera. This was not my path. Even when I was twenty-two, I had a face (and a hairline) made for radio. Being a television reporter seemed an impossibly long way from my job on the graveyard shift writing stories, ripping scripts, and running the teleprompter, among other things.

When a position as a health segment producer opened up, however, Lisa encouraged me to apply. She put in a good word for me with the executive director and news director, who were both a little concerned about putting a twenty-two-year-old dude in charge of a segment that is geared heavily toward a female audience. They both trusted Lisa, however, and that was enough to give me a chance. I took it, and for the first time in my life was able to do real reporting. Well, I was able to go out in the field, conduct interviews, work with a videographer, and write up a package for the anchor who hosted our health segments. I didn't care about the face time, frankly. I was having too much fun with my job.

Getting out into the field instead of working in the newsroom was a game-changing experience, and working with Barry, one of the videographers on staff, provided me with my second mentor. Barry was older than I was, already married with two adorable kids. He was grounded in an industry full of narcissism and unchecked egos, and, like

Lisa, was always calm no matter the breaking news. Barry helped me with everything from my interview skills to dealing with some of the frostier personalities in the newsroom. He treated me as his peer, not some know-nothing punk who'd be gone in six months. And I really appreciated that.

My mentors helped give me a crash course on local news gathering, and when I did ultimately make the transition to reporting, albeit on radio and not TV, it was in large part because of the lessons I learned from them. Just because you're not in class doesn't mean school's not in session. The real world has a lot to teach.

What Would Ward Cleaver Do?

He certainly wouldn't whine about the job market or his need for self-fulfillment; he'd get on a career ladder and climb it for the most important end of all—supporting his family.

9

The Benefits of Getting Fired

lmost any grown man you know has a "the time I got fired/laid off" story. They just don't advertise them. Maybe they'll mention it, in a Toby Keith "How Do You Like Me Now?" boast. But for some guys, the day they got fired is just too heartbreaking to talk about.

An unlucky photographer was fired from Patch.com live on a conference call.* Other staffers at Patch were informed of their dismissal via a recorded message. You hear some of these stories and wonder if some employers are in a sadistic competition to come up with the coldest and most impersonal way of communicating the bad news: Termination notices sent by FedEx. Firings on Christmas Eve. Actor Jeffrey Tambor recalls being interrupted, mid-sentence, while performing a scene on the old 1980s television show *Max Headroom*, that the show was canceled,

---

* Paul Petrone, "The Worst Way to Fire Someone: I Was There," LinkedIn.com, February 17, 2015.

and production was stopping immediately. He didn't even get a chance to finish the sentence!

If you're a Millennial, you might be more focused on finding a job than worried about losing one. But if your situation at work is looking grim, take heart. Getting fired can be a blessing, even if the immediate experience is miserable.

One bit of advice right away: it might seem like a good idea to go out in a blaze of glory, perhaps engaging in a preemptive strike on social media and telling your boss to take this job and shove it. But please don't. Let someone else be the #MoronOfTheMoment on Twitter.

You've just been fired. The most important thing isn't how you feel. The most important thing is finding another job. You'll have a much easier time if there's not a Vine zooming around the Internet of you rapping about your boss.

The much better option is to cast your net far and wide for another job the next morning. And when we say far and wide, we don't just mean looking on Craigslist *and* LinkedIn. We mean looking outside of your comfort zone. Look at every job in the want ads in the local paper. Think about what you can do and not just about what you want to do. What you want to do is earn enough money to maintain your current level of existence. How you do that, as long as it's legal, is really of secondary concern.

You can still focus on a career path, but don't let that focus keep you from paying the bills.

Chances are you've never heard of Mark Lollo. John Feinstein wrote about him in his book *Where Nobody Knows Your Name*, which chronicles a season in Minor League Baseball. Lollo was an umpire. By 2012 he'd risen from umpiring college games to umpiring in Triple-A, even occasionally filling in at a Major League game. But in 2012, just when Lollo was expecting his big break, he was given notice that he wasn't being invited to umpire the following spring. Not in the majors. Not in the minors.

Lollo didn't take to YouTube or Twitter to complain about the injustice of it all. He quietly accepted reality. He contacted the guy who'd given him his first chance to umpire a Major League baseball game, a man whose opinion he trusted, to ask if he'd done everything he could to achieve his dream. He was told he had. And that allowed Lollo to move on. In fact, while Lollo isn't an umpire anymore, he's still very much in baseball (at the time of this writing). In 2014, Lollo landed a job training and evaluating umpires for Minor League Baseball's Umpire Development staff. He's still making a living from baseball, and that's pretty awesome.

 I've only been fired once, and it was from the best meaningless job I ever had. That firing freed me for an actual career that's spanned more than twenty years now. I was working at a video shop owned by a couple who had two sons. The oldest was roughly my age, and it turned out he needed my job more than I did, so I was canned and he took my place. I was crushed. I loved working at the video store. The work was easy, the pay was relatively good, and I got paid to basically watch movies all day. As I said, the best meaningless job I ever had.

After I was fired, I wasn't really sure what I wanted to do. The two most interesting options were working as a cashier at a dairy bar called Braum's or becoming a master control operator at a local TV station. The TV job was obviously much cooler, but Braum's paid better. Ultimately, it wasn't that difficult a choice. Neither paid particularly well, but telling a date that I worked at the NBC station in town sounded much better than "I work at Braum's." I'd done my time in fast food; I was ready to get outside my comfort zone.

This is the "getting fired can be the best thing to ever happen to you" part of the story. The master control operators at the station were mostly lifers uninterested in advancing to other TV production jobs, and there was no shortage of extra work for an eager pair of hands to do. I took advantage of that and quickly became the third man in a three-man production team. I learned a lot from Mike and Richard, my two direct supervisors, but they expected me to show initiative too. They were happy to have someone semi-capable who could perform the less desirable duties, like directing our broadcast of an Assemblies of God service, which meant getting up around 6:30 a.m. on a Sunday morning. While they got to sleep in, I got to direct a multi-camera event from inside a production truck. I realized one Sunday morning that I was still watching a TV at work—only now I was making television, not just renting out videos.

I left that job on my own, because I wanted to leave Fort Smith and return to Oklahoma City. When you quit a job, the "don't be an ass" rule still applies: give your two weeks' notice, be polite, and move on.

Losing your job is hard, but with the right attitude and work ethic, every apparent setback can also be an opportunity. That's the way you should approach it.

 I worked for a few dot-coms, one that was suddenly sold to another dot-com, and then a half year later the bigger fish that ate the small fish laid everyone off and went under. I channeled a bit of frustration about the callousness and coldness of the process into my novel *The Weed Agency*. I watched a large number of my coworkers go into a meeting to get the bad news. And while they were in that meeting, spectacularly unscrupulous non-laid-off workers raided things from their desks. Can you imagine learning the bad news that you're losing your job, and returning to find your desk ransacked? These poor folks were told to clean out their desks, only to find some of their colleagues had already started. Our small band of remaining writers set up a dart board near our office entrance. By frequent dart-throwing we hoped to make our office too dangerous for bad-news-carrying HR staffers to enter.

It didn't work, of course. The pain of being laid off from SpeakOut. com was ameliorated a bit by the fact that we knew it was coming. It was the opposite of a shock. The final months at that place had more ominous foreshadowing than *Twin Peaks*. I remember deciding to go into the office some winter Sunday to print out resumes and cover letters. I came in to find most of my colleagues already there, doing the same thing.

My most painful firing came from a job as a Pentagon correspondent. For two weeks, the job was terrific; the editor was nice and liked everything I wrote. What I didn't notice was the rising stress levels of the other staffers or that my editor's office door was suddenly closed.

[Cue Jaws *theme or appropriate ominous music]*

One morning, my editor called me into his office and informed me that he had been wrong when he hired me; there actually hadn't been money in the budget for my job. Now, you would think this would be the sort of thing the company would straighten out *before* they hired me. But they hadn't, and thus I was getting laid off after two weeks.

For a couple of moments in that meeting, I seemed to think I could *reason* with him that he just couldn't do this sort of thing. It was *unprofessional*! You don't hire someone and then let him go two weeks later without cause! Surely they could find some money from somewhere else in the budget to spare themselves the embarrassment they were feeling at this moment. When it was clear that no, today would be my last day, and that I would be paid for my two weeks, and that would be it, and that he honestly couldn't say when or if the company would have the money to rehire me, then I got angry. Looking back, I wish he had gotten angry as well. He just sat there and took it. He knew his company had screwed up, and there was nothing to be done but apologize. Of course, I was looking for a job again.

Maybe everything happens for a reason; had I remained at that job, there's a pretty good chance I would have been in the Pentagon on 9/11.

The publisher went bankrupt shortly after my departure. The only good news about your employer going under is that you no longer have to worry about the nondisclosure or non-compete clauses in your contract.

By the way, where the heck did this "non-compete" notion come from? What kind of wussy Communist talk is this? If you don't want me competing with you, then you must think I'm good at my job. And if you think I'm good at my job, why are you letting me go?

You can sometimes tell when layoffs are approaching. The regular communication and interaction with management and the higher-ups gets interrupted and goes quiet. There are suddenly a lot more closed-door meetings. Projects get suddenly and mysteriously canceled.

If you work for a big publicly traded corporation, you may want to keep an eye on the company's stock price and what industry publications are saying about your company.

When dark clouds are over your workplace, the best strategy is to keep your head down, work like a madman, and try to make yourself as indispensible as possible. Ask many questions, but spread little gossip. Resist the temptation to grow a beard, put on a fur coat, carry around a broadsword, and ominously whisper to your coworkers, "Brace yourselves. Winter is coming!" like Ned Stark from *Game of Thrones.*

But there is a good chance that employment winter is indeed coming, and heads are gonna roll—thankfully not as badly as poor Ned's did. If you've been in your workplace for a while, you can sense the atmosphere, the rhythms, the normal level of tension, and what's out of the ordinary.

If you do get cut, there's a good chance that after cleaning out your desk, saying goodbye to your coworkers, and trudging to your car, it will be raining cinematically. You will turn on your car's radio, and a song like "It's So Hard to Say Goodbye to Yesterday" or "Where Did We Go Wrong" will play. You'll blow your nose with a half-used Kleenex that was in between the seats. You'll realize that you'll wake up the next workday morning with no place to go.

You'll feel like a failure. Maybe your boss told you you're a failure. Or maybe he said it's not your fault; you can lose your job even if you're good at it.

You didn't deserve this. (Well, most of you.)

There is only one way to survive unemployment: relentless, bottomless, indefatigable determination. It stinks. But you have to turn into a crazed stalker, obsessively pursuing that next perfect job. It's out there. It might be obscured. You might feel like it's hiding from you. You are Samuel Gerard, and your next job is Richard Kimble. And you have to do something every weekday—resumes, look online, call up contacts and ask them if they've heard of any openings, look for freelance or temp work. Despite what your boss just said, you still have a job. That job is *finding your next job.*

You may want to say, "Jim, you're full of crap, you don't practice what you preach when it comes to remaining determined and resolute when times are tough." Guilty. Man, during that stretch of unemployment, I was a mess, the perfect portrait of a shiftless, miserable layabout. All I can say is that you hate in others what you can't stand in yourself. I stayed up until 3 a.m. a lot of nights. I developed an obsessive viewing habit of *Deep Space Nine* reruns, calling up the local affiliate when they aired them out of order. I didn't take care of myself. I ate bad food in portions that would make Adam Richman say, "Whoa, buddy, that's a bit much." I was a surly jerk to my friends. I marinated in self-pity.

Eventually I snapped out of it and found a job at a wire service just as my savings were running out. My friends and family increasingly asked why the hell I hadn't applied for unemployment benefits. I could say it was a bold principled stand, a reflection of my reflexive aversion to government assistance and my affirmation of the need for self-reliance. But the simpler and more accurate answer was that I viewed applying for unemployment insurance as an admission of defeat. Taking some government check would mean that the phone wasn't going to ring today. I was stubborn and depressed, but strangely—probably naively—optimistic that whatever resumes I sent today were going to lead to a good job. A lot of people will dismiss my reaction back then as stupid, but it worked for me.

I urge the "relentless Terminator-like determination" response to unexpected unemployment not because it's easy, but because it's necessary.

As hard as it is to stay as driven after sending out ten, twenty, fifty, one hundred resumes and not getting the returned phone call, there's almost inevitably a payoff to this approach to your hardship. Despair is easier, but it just keeps you there.

What Would Ward Cleaver Do?

Ward had an advantage that you might not have but might want to develop. They didn't talk about networking in his day, but men like Ward Cleaver weren't atomized worker bees, they were part of a community. They knew their neighbors; they belonged to clubs, business-related and otherwise. In the unlikely circumstance that Ward Cleaver lost his job, not only would he work quickly to find a new one, but it's likely that his company's nearest competitor would move quickly to pick him up: Ward Cleavers don't land on the job market every day.

10

Finding Your Vocation

No doubt, there are Millennials who need their sense of entitlement swatted.

In fact, this appears to be a point of consensus among non-Millennials. English teacher David McCullough Jr. became an unexpected social media phenomenon with his 2012 Wellesley High School commencement address that's been viewed on YouTube more than 2.5 million times. McCullough's blunt message to the graduates on their special day was that, in fact, they're not special.

> You are not special. You are not exceptional. Contrary to what your U-9 soccer trophy suggests, your glowing seventh grade report card, despite every assurance of a certain corpulent purple dinosaur, that nice Mister Rogers and your batty Aunt Sylvia, no matter how often your maternal caped crusader has swooped in to save you...you're nothing special....

You see, if everyone is special, then no one is. If everyone gets a trophy, trophies become meaningless. In our unspoken but not so subtle Darwinian competition with one another—which springs, I think, from our fear of our own insignificance, a subset of our dread of mortality—we have of late, we Americans, to our detriment, come to love accolades more than genuine achievement.

In this he echoed perhaps Pixar's finest movie, *The Incredibles*, in which the superpowered family laments the everyone-gets-a-trophy attitude. Their unique powers illuminate the obvious point through exaggeration: just as only they have superstrength, elastic stretching, and freezing powers, only a select few among us are the smartest, the most talented, the strongest, the most unique—and it's silly, self-defeating naiveté to pretend otherwise.

But if the phrase "everyone is special" makes people want to hunt down Barney the Dinosaur and ensure he joins his extinct ancestors, let's just tweak that a bit to read, *everyone is unique.* And from there, let's apply this to what they're capable of doing in the time they have upon this earth. In short, not everyone is great. But there's not a person on this earth who isn't capable of greatness.

Oftentimes, that greatness isn't so visible early in life, or it manifests itself in a quite different way than we expected.

Charles Krauthammer, maybe the world's most brilliant political columnist and certainly one of the most influential voices in Washington, began life as a young man wanting to be a doctor. In his first year at Harvard Medical School, he was paralyzed in a diving board accident and has been in a wheelchair ever since. Work in psychiatry opened doors to the world of public health policy, which led to work in the Carter White House and writing speeches for Walter Mondale—Republican Krauthammer fans, let that sink in for a moment—which led to writing essays for the *New Republic.*

Wrestling and Hollywood superstar Dwayne "The Rock" Johnson played on the University of Miami's championship-winning college football team and dreamed of NFL stardom—until a back injury side-lined him for his senior year. He went undrafted, struggled in Canada's football league, and was finally cut. He returned to the family business of the wrestling circuit and became probably the biggest movie, television, and commercial star to come out of professional wrestling.

Bill Gates dropped out of Harvard. Elvis Costello was a computer programmer. Jerry Seinfeld was written out of his first television role on *Benson*. Mark Cuban was fired from his job as a salesman at a computer store. Albert Einstein was a pretty mediocre patent office clerk. Charles Schulz, creator of "Peanuts," was turned down for a job at Disney. Alan Rickman was a graphic designer and had meager success as a stage actor until he took his signature role in *Die Hard*—at age forty-one.

Everybody who is indisputably "special" was, at one point, nobody special.

If you believe that God—or Fate, or the random combination of two separate sets of genetic material—creates every single person born on earth with something uniquely valuable about them, it creates some far-reaching ramifications. It means everyone has value. Nobody's a waste of space. Everybody's got some talent, some gift they're meant to share with the world.

Maybe people reject this possibility because it demands too much of them; it reminds them that they are only a fraction of what they could be; and it reminds all of us that homelessness, drug addiction, violent crime, and incarceration are social problems that rob us of talents that were not properly employed.

If we accepted that everyone in our world has value, it would have a sweeping impact on our politics. "No child left behind" would be more than a slogan. Every failing school would be regarded as an abomination, a demonic waste of talent, and even schools that churn out mediocrity would be seen as having failed in their duty to get young people to seek out their potential for greatness. The problem of pervasive unemployment would not be limited to putting people on benefits or helping them find jobs, but would guide them to careers that tap their special talents.

You can imagine other far-reaching ramifications. (COUGHabor-tionCOUGH.)

Maybe there aren't any obvious indicators of what makes you unique, special, blessed, and gifted at this moment. But there can be. You are uniquely capable of great achievements. It's called finding your voca-tion, your special calling in life.

 When I was five I wanted to be a paleontologist. Like the vast majority of little boys, I thought dinosaurs were the coolest things ever. I also liked saying the word paleontologist. I dreamed of roaming great des-erts and rugged mountains digging for fossils, discovering new species (like *Camosaurus rex*), and maybe even finding out if the Loch Ness Monster was real. After *Indiana Jones and the Temple of Doom* came out, I decided I wanted to be an archaeologist with a bullwhip to fight off enemies.

As I grew older, the list of things I wanted to be expanded. When I was twelve, I picked up a biography of Edward R. Murrow, and as I read about his reporting from London during the Blitz I became captivated by the power of the microphone.

When parents (my own or a date's mom or dad), or guidance coun-selors, or college applications asked about my future plans, I replied, "I want to be a journalist." And I wasn't lying. Not really. Well, kind of. I did want to be a journalist, but only if my real dream didn't pan out. In my heart of hearts, I didn't want to be a reporter. I really, truly, and desperately wanted to rock.

I'm just old enough that the first years of my adolescence dovetailed with the glorious swan song of the Metal Years. I spent my Friday nights in sixth and seventh grade at the roller skating rink in Norman, Oklahoma, desperately trying to make my feathered hair look longer and hoping that my Ratt T-shirt and the zebra striped bandanna on my thigh made me look like Warren De Martini and not, say, a victim of a horrible safari wound that forced me to use a piece of zebra hide as a tourniquet.* Every fifth song or so the lights would dim and a power ballad would start playing before the roller rink DJ would intone, "Couples skate," or even worse, "Ladies Choice." I was not part of a couple. I was a loner. A rebel. Plus, I couldn't skate backward, so that made skating with a girl an even more daunting proposition.

Every now and then I'd get to go to a concert, which only fueled my desire to become the next Stephen Pearcy. It was gonna happen, and it was gonna rock you like a hurricane. I had my jean jacket with a hand-drawn Metallica logo on the back. I cheered on Dee Snider when he faced down Al Gore and the censorious Parents Music Resource Center in a congressional hearing. Like countless other metal kids my age, I doodled logos for my future bands on the covers and insides of all my school notebooks.** I had all of the desire, and absolutely no ability to play a musical instrument other than the piano (the most un-metal of all instruments). If I couldn't play, I'd have to sing. I'd also need to find other people who had actual musical talent.

It wasn't until high school that I was able to find people my age who actually owned musical instruments, and by then my tastes had changed. R.E.M.'s *Out of Time* turned me from a metal head into a poetry-writing, Homburg-wearing, wannabe Michael Stipe. With my friend Todd on guitar, my friend Joe on the drums (well, a drum, a snare drum; it's what we could afford), and me on a Casiotone keyboard and a Realistic brand microphone from RadioShack, we began to create music. Really, really crappy music.

Oh, we tried. And we could muddle our way through three-chord rockers like the Velvet Underground's "There She Goes Again" and "House of the Rising Sun." We did a not-too-terrible-for-teenagers version of "It's the End of the World as We Know It (and I Feel Fine)." We also tried to write our own songs, all of which were pretty awful.

---

* I'm pretty sure I failed.
** According to my thirteen-year-old self, I was going to front either Gracious Fury or Saintz Alive. I think I was going through a Stryper phase at the time.

After high school Joe headed west, while Todd and I went off to college together. Journalism remained my backup career choice. I was (sadly) way more excited about playing college bars than going to college. We reconstituted ourselves as an acoustic duo called The Almighty Bucks,* learned a lot more R.E.M. songs (as well as the 4 Non Blondes song "What's Up?," which I loathe to this day), and eventually acquired Todd's roommate Len as our bassist and a local musician Neil as our drummer. Finally we were a four piece!

A four piece that went absolutely nowhere, unfortunately. Still, the dream refused to die. Through personal and personnel changes alike, Todd and I continued writing and playing music together. Another four piece formed around our nucleus, with our friend Jonathan on bass and a different Joe on drums. This time we were called Another Engine, after an R.E.M. song, and we played a few club dates around Oklahoma City. We recorded a five-song demo, including the first song I ever wrote about my future wife (we were communicating online and hadn't actually met yet). In February 1997 she flew out to Oklahoma City for a weekend, and our band had a gig that Saturday night. The crowd was good (we played a lot of covers, though no 4 Non Blonde songs), the woman I was trying to impress was impressed, and I even had a chance to sing a couple of songs I'd written about her to her face.

Things were going well for the band, but to my surprise so was my backup plan to be a journalist, since I was now a producer at a local television station. I enjoyed my day job and worked hard at it (after all, it was paying the bills), but I thought it was tiding me over until our band's big break.

Instead, the band had a big breakup. In a matter of months, Jonathan and his wife moved to Texas, Joe left the band, I'd gotten married and was now a father with two kids, and I'd taken a radio job as a beat

---

* The band logo I doodled featured a stuffed and mounted deer head with a halo; yet another band name with a semi-religious reference. Maybe I really wanted to be the next Michael W. Smith, not the next Michael Stipe.

reporter. Music was no longer the most important thing in my life; even when I listened to the radio, it was now Dr. Laura, Rush Limbaugh, and my mentors at the station, Mike McCarville and Jerry Bohnen.

Looking back, my dream career derailed at exactly the right time.

But the dream didn't die entirely. My friend Todd and I managed to spend a few hours a week writing songs; we played a few open-mike nights (without ever promoting ourselves). It was not about a career anymore; it was another way to be creative and to maintain a great friendship.

As it turned out, it wasn't archaeology or rock stardom that I wanted, or even journalism necessarily. What I wanted was a job that allowed me to explore the world around me, to indulge and engage my curiosity, to be creative, to inform and be informed. I'm very lucky that my semi-practical backup plan actually worked. I'm well aware that's not the case for everyone.

It may be that you end up working a job that you tolerate in order to pay for the things you're passionate about. This really isn't that unusual, at least according to a 2013 survey by the firm PayScale, which found that 48 percent of Millennials reported having "low job meaning."* But a boring job can pay for a pretty interesting life, and there's no reason why you have to define yourself by your career.

Moreover, a job doesn't have to be permanent. If you want a job with "value" and "meaning," you'll make that a priority. Just remember, it might take you a while to find that job. In the meantime, paying your bills is meaning enough. With resilience and perseverance, time and effort, you can build from a "pay the bills job" to a "dream job."

In early 2004 I was presented with an opportunity of a lifetime: move to Washington, D.C., and host a live, daily talk show focusing on our right to keep and bear arms. The only drawback was that it meant uprooting my family from the life that we'd established; my wife would

---

* "Gen Y on the Job," PayScale, October 2013, http://www.payscale.com/data-packages/generations-at-work.

have to leave her job, my kids would have to leave their schools and day care, we'd have to sell the house, and we'd be leaving all of our friends behind to start over in a new place. What's more, I wasn't unhappy in my job hosting the morning news show at the AM radio station where I worked, and I'd established a good relationship with advertisers and sponsors. The ratings were good, I had a great mentor in my program director Mike, and there was a really good chance that if I stuck around, I could eventually be the afternoon drive host. Plus, I knew Oklahoma City. I'd grown up there. I loved the city and the community I served, and I'd be leaving right as the city was poised for something of a renaissance.

At the same time, I'd been wondering about my career path. I was comfortable in my job, and there was something appealing about the potential to become a local radio institution, but there was also a part of me that wanted to push myself, to see where my career would take me if I left the safe haven of my hometown. I liked the idea of focusing on the political and cultural fights being waged over our right to keep and bear arms, and the idea of going from my state's capital city to the nation's capital (actually, the studio was located a few miles outside of D.C.) sounded pretty cool to a twenty-nine-year-old.

I took advantage of the opportunity and accepted the job at NRA News. It helped that Mike, my program director, told me I should take the job. The opinion that mattered most, of course, was that of my wife. She had moved from New Jersey to Oklahoma seven years earlier, and now I was asking her to move another fifteen hundred miles to Virginia. She had a house that she loved, friends that she adored, and a job that she liked (and one she did very well). I was asking her to give up her dream for mine, or at least that's what it felt like, and part of me felt crummy and selfish. She'd built a life of her own in Oklahoma City, and I was going to take that away.

I would have understood had my wife told me she didn't want to move; but she said that she had built a life with me, not with a place. That made it a much easier decision. In fact, the hardest part was for the kids; it was a big change for all of them, but especially for my oldest daughter, who was a junior in high school. She spent her senior year in a huge and impersonal high school in the D.C. suburbs. She handled that with more grace and good humor than I would have; she also made a beeline back to Oklahoma for college.

Our career dreams can change, but the point is, whether your job fulfills you or fills you with dread, a meaningful life is always within your reach. I thought my vocation was in music. Actually, it was in radio, and even more than that in being married with kids.

What Would Ward Cleaver Do?

It's pretty obvious that Ward found his vocation when he married June and had two sons, Wally and Theodore ("the Beaver"). Whatever work he did, whatever hobbies he had, his priority, his calling in life, was to be a husband and father.

PART III
Love and Marriage

My most brilliant achievement was my ability to be able to persuade my wife to marry me.

—Winston Churchill

11

Asking Her Out

So there's this guy. And this guy knows a girl. He doesn't know her that well, but every time he sees her there's a little hitch in his breath. They were at a happy hour with some friends, drinking rum and cokes, and debating whether Doogie Howser, M.D., grew up to become House M.D.

He noticed her smile that night, and it seemed she glanced his way on occasion. Was she interested? Should he ask her out?

 Most twenty-something single women we know predict that this fella will follow up with a text or e-mail like this:

"Had fun talking last night. We should hang out sometime. Maybe get a drink!"

Don't do this. This is not asking a woman out. This is the passive-aggressive mating cry of the North American ManChild, and it is a sad and lonely call. Rare is the woman who responds favorably to its forlorn bleating.

If you're truly interested in possibly dating this woman, ASK HER OUT. Call her and say, "Hey, I really enjoyed talking with you the other night. If you're free, can I take you out to dinner? I know a great little farm-to-table/greasy spoon diner/small plate place that I think you'd enjoy."

Be honest, direct, and clear that YOU ARE ASKING HER OUT. You're asking her out because she's interesting. She's attractive, charming, and engaging. You're asking her out because there's a spark, at least on your end. And if you're okay with who you are, then there's no reason not to be confident in your actions.

What about rejection? If the attractive, charming, and engaging woman of your dreams (or at least your daydreams of the past week) says something like, "I had a really good time too! Unfortunately, I'm really tied up with work and don't know when I can get away" or "I had a really good time too, but I have a boyfriend already," what do you do then?

Take it like a man, say thanks, and say you hope to see her soon. That's it.

Now, I won't deny that there's a sting that comes with rejection. But unless you hole up in a cave for the rest of your life, you're going to be dealing with rejection for decades to come, so it's best to develop that tough skin early. Maybe you *will* meet up again at another happy hour. Maybe something will develop over time. Maybe it won't. But the point is, you make the call and then move on.

There's a good chance, of course, she'll respond to your invitation with "That sounds great! Would next Wednesday work?"

But you won't know unless you ask.

There's no reason that a first date has to be awkward, though I've had my fair share. I learned the hard way after watching *Pulp Fiction* that Quentin Tarantino movies aren't exactly great first date experiences. In fact, a trip to the movies is a really lame first date. So is a loud bar.

Basically, any place where you can't really talk to your date is a poor location for your time together. That doesn't mean that the only requirement is a quiet place. Graveyards are a bad choice, unless she's really into vampires and werewolves, for instance. A quiet restaurant or even a picnic at a park is always a good choice. It could be as simple as lunch from a food truck while sitting underneath a shade tree. I think the most important thing is that you're able to talk.

A great first date starts with a great connection, and to have that, you need great conversation with as few awkward silences as possible. That doesn't mean you have to launch into your twenty-minute monologue about politics, religion, your least favorite TV show, the unappreciated genius of your favorite band, or, even worse, a long rambling diatribe that flits from subject to subject without ever allowing for your dinner companion to get a word in edgewise. In fact, please don't do any of that. Instead of bragging about yourself, why not find out more about the incredibly interesting person sitting across from you? Great chemistry can be found through great conversation, after all.

Take the Risk

There are a lot of theories about why dating appears to be dying out among Millennials. There's the "hook up" culture of course, but it should be noted that, at least according to some surveys, there's not really any more casual hooking up than a generation ago, and some evidence that *fewer* college students are sexually active. Along with less dating, there's also less cohabitation and less marriage. You know what we do have a lot more of than we had a generation ago? Online porn.

It may very well be that the ubiquitous nature of online pornography and the relative ease of hooking up for a casual encounter have made dating seem like less of an imperative and more of a chore. In 2011, Davy Rothbart wrote a piece for *New York* magazine about how porn is affecting men's libidos. Porn, he theorizes, may be causing us to detach from our real-life sexual partners, or even replace them in some circumstances.

In talking with a number of guys about their experience with porn, what he found was that many of them, even in their twenties, were losing interest in their real-world sexual partners because porn was sexier, kinkier, and more accessible than their spouse. Most of them felt bad about it, but not enough to quit watching and pay more attention to a real woman instead.*

While Rothbart's article focused on guys who were actively involved in relationships, it stands to reason that single guys might be even more vulnerable to porn's pernicious availability. There's a cost to this far beyond the monthly Internet bill. As Thomas Paine put it in *The Crisis*, "What we obtain too cheap, we esteem too lightly. It is dearness only that gives everything its value." For the first time in human history we can get a reasonable facsimile of sex (or possibly even the real thing) at any hour of the day with little or no work whatsoever. I can't help but wonder if that's leading more and more of us to decide that pursuing or maintaining a real relationship simply isn't worth the trouble.

Among the many user reviews on Amazon.com for Helen Smith's 2013 book *Men on Strike: Why Men are Boycotting Marriage, Father-hood, and the American Dream—and Why It Matters*, a commentator calling himself "FullyAwake" proclaims that he is one of the men on strike, despite believing that "marriage and family are probably the best things you could possibly have in life." Why? Too risky, he says. "One slip up with a woman and your life could be ruined."

Maybe that's true, but life entails risk. It was risky for Cam to marry a woman nearly a decade his senior who already had two kids and whom he had known for less than a year. Without risks, you're not likely to find many rewards in life. You're certainly not likely to find love.

So ask her out. Yes, there's the chance she'll say no. Even if she says yes, there's a slight chance that it could turn out catastrophically bad and your life will be forever ruined. Though I doubt it; forever is a long time. There's also a slight chance that you'll meet someone you know is the

---

* Davy Rothbart, "He's Just Not That into Anyone," *New York* magazine, January 30, 2011, http://nymag.com/news/features/70976/index1.html.

love of your life the moment you see her. The odds are pretty good that a first date will lead neither to catastrophe nor to immediate matrimony but to a good meal and a better conversation. But you'll never know unless you actually try.

Take Your Lumps

There's a scene in an early episode of *The Simpsons* that turns the usual Ward Cleaver fatherly wisdom moment on its head. After life has dealt the kids, Lisa and Bart, a terrible disappointment, Homer turns to them and offers his version of a life lesson: "Kids, you tried your best, and you failed miserably. The lesson is, never try."

Sadly there are some people who actually take this message to heart—if not from Homer, than from life's disappointments and rejections.

Everyone gets rejected at some point. You just don't see it. No exceptions. Brad Pitt got dumped. In the late 1980s, before his big break, then–struggling actor Pitt spent what little money he had to fly to Budapest, where his actress fiancée was working on a film. The night he arrived, she announced the engagement was off and she was in love with the director.

"I spent my night in Budapest, sitting on a bench, smoking, with just a local bum to talk to who couldn't speak English. These are the days and nights you remember when you have success. I returned to America absolutely broke."*

Suddenly your rejections, breakups, and other disappointments don't look quite so bad, huh?

There's an obvious sense of shame associated with being told "you're not good enough," which is understandable; what's strange about the human condition in our modern world is that a lot of us try to act like we never, or almost never, experience it.

---

* Caroline Goddard, "Brad Pitt Talks Breakups," sheknows, April 19, 2011, http://www.sheknows.com/entertainment/articles/828889/brad-pitt-talks-breakups.

Our resumes never list the awful failures that offered hard lessons.* Our first date stories rarely include the dumbest decisions we've ever made. Our pictures on the wall never depict us with expressions of despair, wondering how we're ever going to fix what we've broken. Men brag about their conquests—true, exaggerated, or made up entirely—but rarely discuss their failures.

Most of us succeed at avoiding the topic of our rejections, failures, and mistakes so thoroughly that some people who do experience rejection think there's something uniquely wrong or screwed up about them.

Social media exaggerates this effect. A while back a friend said he hesitated to set up a Facebook account, declaring, "I don't want to show off my entire life to the entire world." But very few Facebook users show off their whole life. They show off only the parts of their life that they want to show off—the victories, the great moments, the smiles. It's like a beer commercial. Our Facebook pages depict our lives as we wish they were.

There are exceptions, of course. Some people don't mind telling the world all about their problems, getting some comfort from the messages of sympathy that pour in. It's easy to become attached to the soothing commiseration of others, and that constant reassurance that you're an unfortunate victim of fate, not responsible for this bad turn of events. Accepting pity is easy. Accepting responsibility is hard.

Then there's "Vaguebooking"—when someone posts messages like "This is just the worst day" or "I can't believe this is happening to me" without any further details. It's hard to shake the suspicion that it is a passive-aggressive test of how quickly everyone responds with concern.

There's a sting that comes with rejection. But it shouldn't be crippling, and the fear of rejection shouldn't cripple us either. And there's some disturbing anecdotal evidence that the entire process of dating is changing out of fear of rejection.

---

* "What was your worst failure in your life so far, and what did you learn from it?" would make a really good job interview question.

Our friend Lisa De Pasquale described this phenomenon in her book, *Finding Mr. Righteous*:

> Rather than actually ask a girl out on a date, they would forward an email to a happy hour or some other function. It's not a date invitation, so there's no fear of rejection by the guy. Girls don't know what to do with this passive invitation.

Apparently it's particularly common among young men in the greater Washington, D.C., area. I suppose when your bosses won't let themselves get nailed down to a clear political position, the underlings won't let themselves get nailed down to a clear position on whether they're asking a girl out.

This is the quintessential "Come on, man!" moment.

Unless we want to go back to a culture of arranged marriages, somebody, somewhere, is going to have to take the initiative and get these relationships started. Yes, there are some women who are willing to ask a guy out. Maybe you'll be one of those lucky men.

We intend no disrespect to your qualities as a man and potential mate, but frankly, you just can't count on this.

Even if you did, that approach to dating, relationships, and marriage means you will end up with the best girl who is brave enough to make the first move (remember, women experience fear of rejection, too!) and selects you out of the crowd of men out there. (Reminder: There are roughly 151 million men in the United States. Even when you toss out those under eighteen, married men, gays, and the senile, you're still going to have to stand out in a crowd.)

Maybe that will turn out okay for you—there are about eighty-eight single men for every one hundred single women in the United States. But you'll admit the odds aren't great.

Alternatively, you can try asking the girl out.

Let's go back to that "forwarded e-mail to happy hour" approach lamented by the young women we know. This doesn't make them feel particularly wanted or desired. The intent is vague: "What is this, a professional networking event? Am I supposed to bring business cards?"

This hapless guy's strategy to minimize the risk of rejection is to make the invitation as unimportant and consequence-free as possible. The problem is you're also saying that *you* are as unimportant and consequence-free as possible.

Think about the message this sends to the girl! *"Eh, it's just an event. It wasn't even important enough to pick up the phone and ask using vocal cords. I'm going to save using those for someone special."* It's a forwarded e-mail. Literally, the only energy expended was to press the "forward" and "send" buttons. The unwritten subtext is, *"The prospect of us spending time together only warrants two mouse clicks' worth of effort."*

The subtext of "eh, I don't really care about this invitation" can easily be interpreted as, "eh, I don't really care about inviting *you*"...or perhaps, "eh, I don't really care about *me*."

You should not see going out on a date with you as a burden you are inflicting on some unlucky attractive woman. If you can't generate some not-so-subtle sense of enthusiasm or excitement or appreciation of an evening out with her, how in the world do you expect her to do the same?

Now imagine if you called her and said, "I've got this after-work happy hour—want to meet there and I'll take you to dinner afterward?"

Suddenly it's much clearer. And then you've got a shot.

What Would Ward Cleaver Do?

In Ward's day, there was no hiding behind electronic media; you actually had to ask a girl out. And he had been in the Navy as a Seabee. Their motto? "Can do!"

12

Getting Married

TICK TICK TICK

Can you hear me? Let me adjust the microphone.

TICK TICK TICK

Any better? No? Okay, let me try again.

TICK TICK TICK

I'm sorry, I'm having difficulty reaching you over the deafening ticking of your girlfriend's biological clock.

A lot of men's hands may well slam this book shut upon hearing those words. It seems like one of the great unspoken sources of tension in relationships—a woman who feels she's in her ideal window of opportunity to have children, involved with a man who's convinced he's just not ready.

As both of us get older, the "forty is the new thirty" philosophy becomes more appealing. We like the idea that our "prime years" could go on much longer than previously thought. Nolan Ryan hurled no-hitters at age forty-four. Michael Jordan scored forty points in a game…at age forty. The late actor Christopher Lee released a heavy-metal album after he turned ninety. And Monica Bellucci is going to be a Bond Girl at age fifty.

But there's one key aspect of human biology that doesn't always play along with our altered life schedule: human reproduction. We're not going to say there's an age at which you should have children, but we are going to say women have good reasons to want to get started in a particular age window.

Before we go any further, let's note that there's an enormous range in human fertility. Once again, those paranoia-driven school health classes may have given some folks the wrong idea. (*"Remember, boys, if you stare at a young woman for too long, you may get her pregnant."*) More than one couple trying to have a baby has chuckled at the irony that after years of being told to take every conceivable—okay, maybe that's the wrong word choice—every *possible* precaution to avoid pregnancy, they engage in repeated marathon bouts of gymnastically challenging unprotected sex and yet, no pregnancy.

You can't force the twists and turns of your life to fit a timetable. But many women are wary about having children after age forty, and they've got some good medical data to back up that perspective. After the fourth decade, it's more difficult to get pregnant and many couples begin to explore the expensive option of in vitro fertilization. Also around that time, the odds increase for a slew of difficult outcomes: miscarriages, Down syndrome, preterm deliveries, problems with the placenta…. We'll refer you to your wife's OB-GYN and other medical books for the full debate. Many women have children later in life and everything turns out fine. But obviously, many women want to complete their family before age forty, and they need a husband who agrees with that timetable.

Why is all this fertility and baby-making talk in a marriage chapter? Because many people, including many women, envision their lives with a marriage first and kids second. Biology gives women a deadline—if not a firm one, then a blurry one, and they work backward; if the last child is born around age thirty-nine or forty, then a preceding child or children have to be born in the preceding years. Which means marriage would ideally occur some stretch before then.

Ideally, you and your girlfriend can have an honest discussion about these issues.

Most young men, even young husbands, don't think about fatherhood very much, outside the context of trying to avoid it. (*"What do you mean, you're late?"*) Once again, my suspicious eye turns to those middle school and high school sex-ed classes, where the catastrophic consequences of teen pregnancy are drummed into the minds of teenage boys in a near-Orwellian fashion. We probably shouldn't blame the health teachers; the heavy-handed techniques are a desperate attempt to shake those teenage boys out of their daydream of impregnating the teenage classmate sitting next to them.

Maybe we need some sort of society-wide class reunion, when men are getting into their late twenties, where their old health teacher will show up and say, "Okay, *now* it's perfectly fine to have unprotected sex and get your wife pregnant." No demonstrations please, Mr. Virgil.

So You're Ready to Pop the Question . . .

We're very pro-marriage guys. So on behalf of young men out there, let us declare loudly, here and now, if society wanted young men to be more enthusiastic about getting married, it would lower the "entry fee" considerably. Oh, sure, there's no *official* entry fee,* but society imposes pretty clear expectations. If you get down on one knee and offer a ring from a box of Cracker Jacks, you'll either get a "no" or a lot of quizzical looks from her friends and family later.

That rule of thumb that an engagement ring should cost about two months' salary? That came from an advertising campaign by the

---

* Besides the marriage license fee, of course. The state of Minnesota charges couples $115 for a marriage license! They knock it down to $40 if you complete twelve hours of "premarital education." Doesn't every moment with your fiancée count as some form of "premarital education"?

De Beers diamond cartel back in the 1930s,* and must rank as one of the most effective advertising messages of all time. Ever since, when it comes time to pop the question, we run to the jewelers with wheelbarrows of cash and scream, "TAKE MY MONEY!"

Yes, it should be a ring that pleases her. Yes, it will be on her hand for the rest of her days (or at least that's the plan). But it should be a ring with a cost that makes financial sense. Someday later in life, when you get the big promotion or win the lottery, you can upgrade.

This is a circumstance where a little flexibility on the part of young women who dream of a happy marriage would be appreciated. If we want to lament that *Maxim* cover starlets and adult entertainment stars create unrealistic expectations in the minds of young men, let's save a little cultural teeth-grinding for those bridal magazines that amount to wedding porn and the cable shows that seem to celebrate "bridezillas."

You can make a case that young men's difficulty in getting married is a giant threat to world peace. In most of the Middle East, it's very difficult for a young man to get married if he doesn't have a job that pays enough to support himself and a home of his own. Because good-paying jobs for young men are rare, a lot of young men have no real interaction with women and no real prospect for marriage and settling down...easy pickings for the apocalyptic ramblings of the radical imam down the street who's promising seventy-two virgins in the afterlife.

Listen up, wedding industry: if you make it more expensive to get married, then the terrorists win.

According to a 2013 Gallup poll,** 14 percent of Millennials who aren't married say it's because of financial concerns. That seems to be reflected in the 66 percent of Millennials making less than $30,000 who say they want to get married yet are single. Among those making somewhere

---

* Laurence Cawley, "De Beers Myth: Do People Spend a Month's Salary on a Diamond Engagement Ring?," BBC News, May 16, 2014, http://www.bbc.com/news/magazine-27371208.
** Frank Newport and Joy Wilke, "Most in U.S. Want Marriage, but Its Importance Has Dropped," Gallup, June 20–24, 2013, http://www.gallup.com/poll/163802/marriage-importance-dropped.aspx.

between $30,000 and $75,000, 25 percent are married but 59 percent would like to be enjoying wedded bliss.

One of the advantages of marriage is that two can live almost as cheaply as one. Rent is shared, as are utilities. Some of that might be offset by the marriage penalty in taxes, but if you're poor it's not much of an issue. Yes, you could shack up together, but that's ultimately just a housing situation with benefits. What you're looking for is a marriage, and it's perfectly okay to struggle at first. In fact, it's normal. We're surrounded with cultural cues to be extravagant, and it would not be surprising if fewer people are getting married in part because of what weddings have become.

Let us put it bluntly. If you can afford a $100,000 wedding with live doves and a cascading fountain of single barrel whisky, awesome. Please send us an invitation. But never, and we mean never, go into debt to pay for your wedding (or your kid's wedding for that matter).

The wedding website TheKnot.com says that the average cost of a wedding is now a whopping $30,000 (honeymoon not included).* In Washington, D.C., it's closer to $40,000. In Manhattan the typical wedding is closer to $87,000. This is nuts. It's a simple truth: your wedding day will be special, no matter how much or how little money you spend on it, as long as your marriage is special to you.

The Case of the Missing Preacher

We spent less than $300 on our wedding, and my wife and I have been married nearly twenty years. We've bought more than that in alcohol for some of our anniversary parties, and we still look back on our wedding day with incredibly warm memories.

We paid $75 for our justice of the peace (an ancient man who was incredibly nice but bore an unfortunate resemblance to the creepy

---

* Melanie Hicken, "Average Wedding Bill Hits $30,000," CNN, March 28, 2014, http://money.cnn.com/2014/03/28/pf/average-wedding-cost/.

undead preacher from *Poltergeist II*), and my betrothed bought a white dress on clearance at a local department store for $30. I came straight from work, and wore khakis and a shirt and tie. My wife baked our wedding cake and made some desserts for our reception (held at the duplex into which I had moved her and the kids until we were married), which brought the total close to $200. In addition to our marriage license, my soon-to-be wife needed a form of identification, and her driver's license from New Jersey had expired, so she ended up buying a fishing license (cheaper than a driver's license, and she wasn't driving my car at the time) in order for us to get our marriage recognized by the state.

Our parents were both mad at us, because they thought we were rushing into a terrible mistake, so it was a small affair. Her dad was nice enough to send flowers, which we used for her bouquet. There wasn't a single acquaintance at our wedding, just close friends.

Though we were getting married in a public park, we refused on ideological grounds to pay the required fee (I hope the statute of limitations has run out, but if not I suppose I stand ready to answer for my civil disobedience). We made a tactical matrimonial strike on an unoccupied gazebo in a garden spot void of other wedding parties or people, and waited for the justice of the peace.

Unfortunately, he was nowhere to be seen at the appointed hour. Only my soon-to-be-wife and I knew what he looked like, so I ran through the park in the August heat until I finally found the old man shuffling along a path near a creek.

"Rev..er..end Fish..er..," I gasped. "Over…here!"

He looked up and smiled, and I started to lead him back to the gazebo. Suddenly (and I wish I was only joking about this), a couple of young guys wearing tuxedos appeared on the bridge behind us.

"Hey," one of them shouted. "Hey, that's our preacher!"

I honestly had no idea what to do. At any moment, I expected the Park Police to arrive and ask me for my permit. I would be hauled away to jail on my wedding day. My new job as a reporter for the local news radio station would vanish. And my wife was, at that very moment, literally waiting at the altar for me to arrive with the good reverend.

I tried to explain that, no, this was my justice of the peace, but they were unconvinced. To this day, I have no idea why they didn't believe me. Who on earth would lie about that? The octogenarian pastor seemed just as happy to go with the tuxedoed men as with me, which didn't help. It wasn't until another couple of tuxedoed members of the permitted wedding party appeared on the horizon and shouted that their preacher had been found that they let us go.

Is it any wonder that after all that I forgot the wedding vows I had written, and had to make them up on the fly?

The point is, your day will be memorable because it's the day you start your life with the person you want to spend the rest of your life with. It's like no other day on this planet regardless of how much money you spend on it. To me it seems silly to make it a fairy tale day. Let it be about the love in your heart, not the money in somebody's bank account (or, more likely, credit card balance or bank loan). There will be plenty of memories to treasure without being serenaded by the original cast of the *Jersey Boys* during your first dance.

At least one study backs me up. In 2014, researchers Andrew M. Francis and Hugo M. Mialon from Emory University surveyed three thousand folks who were married, and they found that while having a high household income increases your chances of a strong marriage, "spending $1,000 or less on the wedding is significantly associated with a decrease in the hazard of divorce," while spending more than $20,000 "is associated with an increase in the hazard of divorce."* Maybe that's because the high rollers are emphasizing the wrong things.

Interestingly, Francis and Mialon also found that strong marriages correlate with attending church, having a child with your spouse, having

---

* Andrew M. Francis and Hugo M. Mialon, "'A Diamond Is Forever' and Other Fairy Tales: The Relationship between Wedding Expenses and Marriage Duration," *Social Science Research Network*, September 15, 2014, http://papers.ssrn.com/sol3/papers.cfm?abstract_id=2501480.

a good number of people at your wedding, and going on a honeymoon. A big ring and a fancy wedding, on the other hand, don't seem to help and may even hurt. So focus on what really matters, not the day of your wedding, but your commitment in marriage.

The Truth about Weddings

Congratulations, you're engaged! Now stay out of the way.

In a better world, weddings would indeed be partnerships, and the bride and groom would go through each major decision in a generous spirit of compromise. But for some reason, the world has decided "it's her day." She gets to be the only one wearing white; you're wearing the same tuxedo as a half-dozen other men up in front of the chapel/church/synagogue/public park. It's as if you're leading an assembly line of penguins.

I hope you've begun gathering intelligence about your bride-to-be's views on weddings beforehand. I completely concur with Cam's points about wedding debt, especially when you keep in mind a good portion of the day will fly by in a blur. It doesn't need to be an Olympic opening ceremony.

Figure out what both of you really need to make your wedding day special, and cut the chaff from the wheat. Your beautiful bride-to-be deserves a wonderful, unforgettable, happy day. What she shouldn't expect—nor should you—is "the happiest day of your life." Talk about putting pressure on yourself! Dispel that notion every chance you get, because it's inherently declaring that it's all downhill from here.

I hate to break it to you, but the day isn't really about you guys. And it may very well end up being a seesaw day of highs and lows, of cheer and stress, of laughing and ah, crap, Uncle Leo is drunk again. Once, in human civilization, weddings were happy gatherings celebrating the union of two souls and the beginning of a new family. Now we've decided they're an opening endurance test of an engaged couple, a marathon of stress and Byzantine logistical details that need to be worked out to the satisfaction of way too many people.

I realize we're swimming upstream in our culture; a vast white-lace conspiracy has decreed that weddings must be ludicrously expensive; brides should be encouraged to get in touch with their inner demanding toddler; the springs of twenty-somethings and thirty-somethings must become can-you-top-this competitions of ostentatious displays of conspicuous consumption—Donald Trump vs. Liberace.

If you're contemplating a "destination wedding," don't. I'll skip over a long series of profanities and just clarify that when you say, *"We're getting married in Hawaii!"** all your friends hear is, *"I've decided what you're doing with your savings and your vacation days!"* Sure, maybe you have always dreamed of getting married on the beach in Oahu, and for you, that happy moment is worth the cost. But your potential best man, maid or matron of honor, groomsmen, and bridesmaids haven't always dreamed of shelling out for airfare and hotel and tuxedo rental and dress purchase to go to the beach and watch you get married. Unless your aim is to get a lot of invited guests to have to politely decline, save the fun exotic travels for the honeymoon.

If you, as a groom, really want to have a say in the details of the wedding, then prioritize—figure out what really matters to you and on what issues you're willing to say "that's fine." Do you really have a strong opinion on centerpieces? As the groom, one of your traditional duties is to plan the honeymoon, which is actually a lot more fun.

You may think of the honeymoon as your reward for surviving the wedding. Just try not to say at the conclusion of the wedding, "We've now shared a very special moment with all of you, and we've never felt so close. Now we can't wait to get on a plane and get an entire continent away from all of you people, so we can go and have sex in peace."

---

* This assumes you don't live in Hawaii, nor is it the hometown of the bride or groom.

My wife and I were the first in our circle of friends to get married, which meant we were the guinea pigs. As you attend and participate in weddings, you learn parts you like and don't like.

If you have a head table, you can only talk to the people on your left and your right. If your table is a circle, you can at least theoretically talk to more than one person.

One of our friends had the groomsmen—which included me—have some special dance with the bridesmaids—which didn't include my wife. This arrangement would not be my first choice. I'm a self-conscious dancer, while my wife might as well be Jennifer Beals in *Flashdance*. If I absolutely have to go on the dance floor in front of a lot of people, I want to get credit for doing so with my wife.

I had all three of my groomsmen give toasts; natural hams, they all excelled at them. There's nothing wrong with multiple toasts if they're quick—funny, funny, funny, funny, sweet, end. If any of your relatives have the public speaking instincts of Fidel Castro, warn the DJ or band to have a version of the Oscar time-to-get-off-the-stage music ready to go on your signal.

The dance between the father of the bride and the bride is always sweet. The dance between the mother of the groom and the groom is tougher, because there aren't a heck of a lot of songs that are (A) about love, but not romantic and (B) danceable for the dance-challenged guy like myself and sweet old mom.

Looking back, my wife and I have only the regret that we went along with a couple concepts out of loyalty to tradition that we thought were necessary, and we've concluded we didn't need them at all.

Nobody smushed cake in each other's face at our wedding.

I can only assume that tradition came from divorce lawyers who asked, "Hey, how can we ensure a marriage gets off on the wrong foot immediately?"

"Okay, people, our caseload is getting thin, we need some ideas to sow marital discord early on. Let's go around the room, just say the first idea that pops into your mind—Wilkins, whaddya got?"

"Um, uh, have the bride and groom smash pieces of expensive cake in each other's faces, while everyone's taking pictures, when they're wearing some of the most expensive clothes they'll ever wear, and she's spent half the day completing her makeup and hair!"

"Love it! Let's start talking this up as a fun, loveable, harmless tradition!"

But cake-smushing is small potatoes compared to the Freudian psychosexual public ritual involving the bride's garter.

Tossing the garter—where the hell did this twisted tradition come from? Everyone has just gathered in a church to pledge their love for each other before God and everyone they know. The bride is wearing white, and the only reference to sex so far has been the always uncomfortable reading of "My lover is like a swift gazelle or a young stag" from Song of Solomon during the ceremony. And then, all of a sudden, everyone— Grandma, Aunt Edna, Uncle Leo—get together and watch the groom try to get to third base under the wedding dress. What the hell? *"Hey, bring over the young nieces and nephews, make sure they get a good look at this!"*

(I looked it up and found out this is a European tradition. Figures.)

As if all of this wasn't bizarre and embarrassing enough, the groom then tosses the garter to the single male guests. Now, I'm a pretty traditional, old-fashioned guy, but this practice feels like it goes back to cavemen—or at least the Vikings. Why am I sharing my wife's lingerie? Why am I sharing my wife's lingerie *in front of everyone I know, including elderly relatives*? Under what other circumstances would this not be creepy and weird? Try this at Thanksgiving, and see how long it takes until someone calls the cops.

"Look! Fellow men! I have determined that my bride wore lace high upon her thigh! I have removed it, and I will toss it to the mass of ye rampaging jackals, and you are to claw each other for the right to hold my beloved's dainty undergarment!"

The bride tosses the bouquet. Then—as if wedding traditions were put together by some twisted reality television show producer—the guy who caught the garter is supposed to put the garter onto the leg—thigh and points north—of the woman who caught the bouquet. Ooh, forced sexual contact between random strangers! Quick, gather around all the distant relatives and coworkers! Take pictures!

How wrong can this go? Well, I remember one wedding where my good friend caught the garter—I had gotten married and was quite happy to be able to opt out of the Larry Flynt–sponsored aerodynamic matchmaking ritual—and the bouquet was caught by...a twelve-year-old girl who had run out, wanting to catch the bouquet and not really understanding the connotation.

Awk-ward.

At that wedding, they thankfully skipped the second half of that bizarre, twisted tradition.

It's one tradition to drop.

What Would Ward Cleaver Do?

He did it—he got married (to his high school and college sweetheart).

13

Advice for New Husbands

 Billy Crystal declares in *When Harry Met Sally* that "When you realize you want to spend the rest of your life with somebody, you want the rest of your life to start as soon as possible."

Well, guess what? It's started.

Wise rabbis, priests, and ministers often say that a marriage isn't just bringing together two souls, it's bringing together two families. Not to mention two sets of furniture—and a roommate.

Some of this is great. You've met the love of your life, and you've wanted her around 24/7; now you've got her. You can fall asleep on the couch together, and take your time with lazy weekend breakfasts. Suddenly everything in your new home is a shared battle—noisy neighbors, rent hikes, the clogged sink. In a successful marriage, there's a sense of you and your loved one taking on the rest of the world together.

Some of this, though, is fraught with peril. All of the tensions and issues and potential landmines of living with a roommate are now applicable to the woman you love, the most important person in your life.

You'll be amazed at the sort of issues that arise, each one a seemingly small issue that can, at almost any point, blow up into a significant conflict and ruin your plans for a nice dinner, a movie, and some nookie that evening. Did you leave the toilet seat up? Your nice romantic weekend is gone, you fool. You may have a shot at détente by Monday.

When putting on a new roll of toilet paper—God help you if you leave your beloved a toilet without toilet paper!—do you have the paper hang over or under? (A little-known fact, this over-or-under dispute is actually what set off the conflict between the Hatfields and McCoys.)

Do you squeeze the toothpaste from the bottom or middle of the tube? The bottom, obviously, unless you're some sort of inefficient philistine with no sense of toothpaste-maximization—*not that either of us married one*! Not that we *mind* re-squeezing it and rolling it up from the bottom every morning!

In what drawer does each kitchen tool go? (This fight is actually somewhat moot, because when your parents or in-laws visit, they will put those instruments back where *they* think they should go. Hell is a house full of microbrew bottles and an inexplicably missing bottle opener.)

At its very best, daily life can become a negotiated division of labor: When there's a bump in the middle of the night, she gets the reassurance you'll get up to see what it was. When you're sick, she'll bring you tissue boxes, orange juice, and hot bowls of soup. When there's a big spider, you'll be there to squash it. That too-tight jar lid? All yours.

Marriage is actually easier if you and your loved one have a yin-and-yang dynamic—different strengths, different preferences. We're a bit wary when a couple insists they're perfect together because they "have so much in common." Your spouse isn't supposed to be a clone of you; you're supposed to have offsetting strengths, weaknesses, perspectives, and ideas. She's a woman, after all, and you're a man; you're different, and that's good; it's literally what makes life possible, not to mention more fun.

Things That Go ZZZZZ in the Night

Before I was married, I foolishly assumed that living with my wife wouldn't be *that* different from having a roommate. Well, I knew it would be very different in some very important ways (cisnormative dude that I am), but I figured that when it came to the day-to-day stuff like paying bills, dividing up chores, and just generally occupying the same enclosed space with another human being, the fact that I had roommates before would prepare me for the adjustment. I was wrong, and mostly for the better.

First off, you may share an apartment with a roommate, but you're likely not sharing a bed. Learning someone's bed-iquette takes time, but it also takes being comfortable with the person you're sleeping with. I come from a long line of loud snorers on both sides of my family. One of my former roommates would fall asleep with headphones on every night, usually opting to drift off to Smashing Pumpkins instead of Snoring Cameron.

My wife, however, doesn't fall asleep listening to music. She doesn't have to. As it turns out my wife can fall asleep roughly thirty seconds after telling me good night and turning off her bedside light. I've *never* been able to fall asleep that easily, so it made it much easier for her to deal with my snoring, because she rarely heard it. I, on the other hand, was able to hear *her* snoring. Not only could I hear it, it was right next to me. At least my roommates had been all the way across the apartment from me when I was buzz-sawing my way through the Dreamland Forest.

Through trial and error I learned the best way to deal with her snoring was to gently try to get her to shift her sleeping position, which would usually give me a couple of minutes respite so I could fall asleep. Some of the errors I committed in the research phase of Operation Silent Sleep included waking her up to tell her she was snoring (spectacularly bad idea) and tickling her side to get her to move (she reflexively lashed out and smacked my nose with her elbow).

Every now and then I'd go to bed before she did, and my wife had her own learning curve in dealing with my snoring. We both figured out that the main objective was to get the other person to change their sleeping position without actually waking them up. Our standard defense against spousal snoring became a gentle but firm push applied to the nearest shoulder of the spouse, increasing slightly in pressure until they rolled over. It works pretty well. Other occasions might lend themselves to the brutal simplicity of yelling "There's a spider on your face!" at your sleeping partner.*

Snoring is one thing, but before you can snore you have to sleep, and that likely means several other adjustments. For some people, like my wife, deciding who's going to sleep on which side of the bed is a big issue. For me, having a bed that wasn't simply a mattress on the floor was a bigger deal. I let her take the right side of the bed, and we went to Goodwill that weekend and bought a Hollywood frame and a used box spring. That was an easy adjustment. Getting used to her morning routine, on the other hand, was really tough.

I'm not exactly a morning person, but once I'm up, I'm up. My wife, on the other hand, likes to ease into the day. If we have to be awake at 7 a.m., for instance, the alarm will go off at 6:40, then 6:49, and again at 6:58. I mentioned earlier my wife can fall asleep within seconds, so this system works perfectly for her. For me, it meant getting up about twenty minutes earlier than I really needed to get out of bed. Keep in mind that I was usually falling asleep after my wife as well, which meant that most nights I'd get anywhere from thirty to forty minutes less sleep than she

---

* When conducting the "There's a Spider on Your Face" maneuver, start by slowly tickling your spouse's face with the tips of your fingers. Do this two or three times if possible before bellowing as loud as you can about the spider. This will help ensure that you don't hear any snoring for the rest of the night from your bed on the living room couch. Remember, always have your smartphone recording before you begin. And don't be an amateur. Good lighting is key to capturing the facial expression of your spouse. Also, invest in a good case for your smartphone so it doesn't break when thrown to the floor.

was getting. That might not seem like much, but over time it can add up. By my estimates, in our eighteen years of marriage my wife has racked up more than 197,000 minutes of sleep than I've managed. That's more than four months of extra slumber!* No wonder my wife looks younger than me.

Beyond the bedroom there are more adjustments in store. It's likely that your décor will change, for example. My wife's brother was a painter, and when we married she moved several rather large canvases into our rather small apartment, where they fought for wall space with my posters of the movie *Clerks* and the band R.E.M. And for whatever reason, my wife wasn't interested in the perfectly acceptable couch that my roommate Todd and I had curb-picked months earlier. Sure, there was a little stuffing coming out of a couple of cushions, and there was a mysterious stain on the back of the couch, but you couldn't even see it if you pushed the couch against the wall. It didn't smell much, except on dank rainy days when there was a musty, old-man funk that seemed to emanate from the plaid fabric.

I don't miss that couch, and I couldn't tell you what happened to my R.E.M. posters, though I suspect they disappeared in a spring cleaning purge or were sold at a yard sale. The walls in our house now are full of pictures of our family (along with my brother-in-law's paintings, my 1974 Boston Red Sox pennant, and a framed poster for my old band). Our couch still smells a little funky at times, but that's usually because of teenage boys, not the ghost of the old man who left his couch at the curb.

As it turns out, I probably needed to make some adjustments, and not just with my furnishings. When I was single, the contents of my refrigerator generally consisted of a package of bologna, a package of cheese, a jar of mayonnaise, and some soda and beer. My pantry

---

* My wife disputes this math and also points out that my calculations do not take into account things like her waking up in the middle of the night and not being able to fall asleep again because of my snoring and the midnight feedings of our three youngest kids when they were breast-feeding. My contention is that if I wasn't so sleep deprived my calculations would have been more precise.

contained a few packages of mac and cheese, canned soup, and ramen noodles. When my mom came to visit for the first time, she immediately went shopping and returned with frozen vegetables, fresh fruit, and a package of multivitamins. The veggies were there when I left, though the fruit did get eaten and I remembered to take my vitamins at least twice a week. I'm convinced those vitamins were the only things keeping me from getting scurvy during my bachelor days.

My wife, on the other hand, could flat-out cook. She knew how to stretch a budget too. Being a poor single mom didn't mean she bought the cheapest frozen pizza and fish sticks to feed her kids. Well, okay, it meant she bought more than just the cheapest frozen pizza and fish sticks. Actual flour. Rice, and not in an Uncle Ben's box. Frozen vegetables appeared in our freezer, and steamed veggies appeared on our dinner plates. I discovered that chicken came in something other than nugget form. It's amazing how quickly you can get used to sitting down to a hearty home-cooked dinner. Those expectations were usually exceeded, with one spectacular exception.

Cam's Christmas Story

We married in August, and a few months later the triple-digit days had disappeared and the winter winds howling across the Oklahoma prairie rattled the thin-paned windows of the upper floor of the rambling and somewhat dilapidated duplex we lived in. We had a magnificent oak that grew near the home and provided much-needed shade in the summer, but at this time of year its branches pointed skyward like a hundred accusatory fingers, wagging at the wind that had stripped it naked.

Inside our tiny apartment, however, it was bright and cheery. A small tree stood decorated in the corner of our living room, and our dog Buttercup lay sleeping in the warm glow of the electric lights. The wrapping paper had been gathered and thrown away, and our kids were happily playing with their new Christmas toys. It was a perfectly Rockwellian scene, and I hearkened back to *A Christmas Story*, one of my favorite movies growing up. I had always identified with Ralphie, but now I was

The Old Man. This was my first Christmas as a husband and father, and it felt good. It felt right. It felt…like I was hungry. It was growing late. When was my wife going to start cooking Christmas dinner?

I had gained roughly twenty pounds in the four months that we'd been married (and I would balloon even larger in the months to come). It was simple food, but it was prepared exquisitely. I swear a good portion of that twenty pounds was gained on Thanksgiving that year. We had a small turkey and the most amazing stuffing I had ever tasted. Add in sweet potato casserole, mashed potatoes and real gravy, homemade rolls, green beans, and a chocolate cake and a pumpkin pie. And now we were going to get to eat it all again for Christmas. Only I didn't smell anything cooking.

I found her in our bedroom, curled up on the mattress that was no longer on the floor, reading a book. When I asked about our Christmas feast, she looked up at me with some confusion, then growing horror, and her eyes grew wide.

See, her Christmas tradition was to go to her dad's house, where he would cook a big dinner for everyone. Only problem was, he was fifteen hundred miles away. My Christmas tradition was usually to eat whatever food was offered to me, so it never crossed my mind to inquire about our Christmas plans. We both simply forgot about dinner. My wife was crestfallen. I wrapped my arms around her and told her it was okay. We could eat Chinese food.

"I will NOT eat Chinese food on Christmas," she flatly stated. "Let's just get in the car and see what's open."

And so we did. Bundled up against the winter cold, we packed ourselves into my 1992 Mercury Topaz and headed off in search of an inn that would give us shelter and a turkey dinner. As we cruised the near-empty boulevards, we saw restaurant after restaurant dark and shuttered for the night. Well, Hunan Garden was open, and had a pretty good crowd, but the icy stare from my wife sealed my decision not to point it out. After a good twenty minutes of driving, with the grumbles of complaint rising from the backseat, we saw a beacon of fluorescent light in the darkness.

"No!" my wife said emphatically, before I could even inquire.

"Honey," I started.

"Don't 'honey' me, Cameron. I am not spending my Christmas dinner at Hooters!"

I wheeled into the parking lot.

"Look," I said emphatically. "You don't want to eat at a Chinese restaurant. Okay. I get it. But there aren't any other restaurants open that we've seen. So, it's either Hunan Garden or Hooters. Or we can go eat sandwiches at home."

Let me state for the record here that I truly had no ulterior motive other than hunger. If Golden Corral had been open, we would have been merrily stuffing ourselves in the buffet line. But it was growing late, everyone was getting hungry and cranky, and a decision had to be made.

And so it was. We marched into Hooters, a steely look in my wife's eyes and huge grin stretching the cheeks of my six-year-old son's face (who, now that I think about it, was pretty much at eye level to quite a few cheeks in that restaurant). This was his first time in a Hooters, and not coincidentally, the last time my wife ever set foot in one.

The meal itself was fine. As you can imagine, it wasn't exactly a full house that evening, and so the servers paid plenty of attention to us (especially the cute kid with the missing front tooth). My wife, though, was quietly continuing to stew. After we paid our check and were walking out to the car, I noticed tears trickling down her cheek.

"I wanted it to be perfect," she sobbed. "It was our first Christmas together. How could I be so stupid and forget dinner?!"

I reminded her that I, too, had forgotten all about it, and it wasn't her fault. This was the first Christmas where neither of us was with our parents. We were doing it by ourselves for the first time. We were bound to make a couple of mistakes. Besides, I told her, in a way this was the perfect ending to our first Christmas.

My wife expressed her skepticism, but I pressed forward.

"Think about it," I said. "If everything had gone as planned, we'd only have the usual memories of a Christmas dinner around the table. We have plenty of years ahead of us for those memories. This was our first Christmas, and we'll never forget it."

She laughed for the first time in hours, even if it was a bit forced.

I offered her my arm and she slid her hand into mine as we walked back to the car on the calm December night. It did take a few years, but eventually she came around and could view that night with a smile. The next year we also had a fantastic Christmas dinner of London broil, baked potatoes, veggies, and a homemade pie. Nothing that even remotely resembled a chicken wing could be found at the table.

With any big transition, there's always a period of adjustment, and living with your spouse is no exception. That settling-in period can be awkward at times, but the first few months of marriage aren't called the honeymoon period for nothing. It seems you find out something new about your spouse every day, or maybe that's just a byproduct of marrying someone within six months of meeting in person. Enjoy the moment, stay curious about your spouse, be able to adjust, and you might be able to extend that honeymoon period for quite a while. At least as long as you don't employ the "There's a Spider on Your Face!" anti-snoring trick.

What Would Ward Cleaver Do?

Ward Cleaver would be more likely giving advice than taking it. What can we say? Ward Cleaver was a stud.

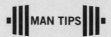

Consult Your Trusted Advisor

In his book *The Alphabet versus the Goddess: The Conflict between Word and Image*, Leonard Shlain offers the theory that the term "sleep on it"—as in waiting until you've had a good night's rest when facing a big decision—originally meant more than just letting your subconscious wrestle with your unresolved question during a good night's sleep. Shlain examines cultures going back to prehistory and notes that most ruling men had two realms where they sought counsel: first in their royal court, from other men, standing or sitting while fully clothed, and then in their bedchamber at night, from their wife (or concubine), naked, reclining. In that second chamber, a ruling man encountered the feminine perspective. Whether he overtly heeded it or not, the process of that secret unofficial advisor—the power behind the throne—undoubtedly influenced the thinking of the ruling man.

Fast-forward to today, and you will find that your wife is undoubtedly your most trusted advisor—or certainly should be—and that these conversations tend to occur late at night, when all the business of the day is done.

14

Owning a Home

 A few years down the road, you may find yourself tiring of renting and eager to buy your own place—or, more likely, you and the Mrs. are feeling ready for that step.

The process of home-buying is a wonderful lesson in how little most of us think about real estate—and as a result of this, we're happy, well-adjusted people. Buying a home was once a technical, complicated, and headache-inducing process, but now thanks to the efforts of realtors, the experience of homeowners during the housing boom and bust, the influence of HGTV, and a ton of federal, state, and local regulations, it's now an even more technical, complicated, and migraine-inducing process. A quality home can make it all worthwhile, but at some point, you will begin to wonder if you've unfairly discounted a nomadic existence.

Why is buying a home turning into your own personal logistical challenge on par with the Berlin Airlift? For starters, there are these wonderful websites like Zillow that, in their opinion, provide a reasonably accurate calculation of a home's selling price. The site's formula is a complicated, secretive algorithm, but it appears to be something like this:

1. Begin by calculating the average price of similar-sized homes that have sold in the past year in that neighborhood.
2. Add *a giant sum of money* to that total.
3. Presto! You have the current market value.

The "giant sum of money" is perhaps a zillion, which would help explain the name.

A disturbing number of people have plugged their home into one of the sites and promptly leaped out of their chair to do the happy dance, as the real estate website has just given them a projected sales price that will allow them to finance that vacation property in Aruba. Sometimes the seller's flesh-and-blood realtors will urge them to adjust the price downward a bit, sometimes they won't. Once someone has been told that they can sell their house at a price that will allow them to live the lifestyle of the Sultan of Brunei, they're quite reluctant to let go of that dream.

Thus, as you tour the open houses—all too often, scheduled for 1 p.m. on Sundays, because apparently the entire real estate world hates football fans—you will find yourself in the presence of an excruciatingly cheery realtor or realtor assistant who seems to think that you're eager to sign over a five-, a six-, or even a seven-figure sum just because they put out a dish of candy that they couldn't give away last Halloween.

You and your beloved, who's got her heart set on a fireplace, a parking space, and a gas stove, will walk around, trying to envision how the place would look with your furniture in place of the seller's, or, in some cases, the painfully generic staging furniture. Staging furniture is designed to work in every room, which means it aims to have absolutely nothing distinctive about it. It appears to be made up of tables and chairs that witnessed mob crimes and had to be ushered into the home furnishing equivalent of the Federal Witness Protection Program. It's so determined to not conflict with any existing décor that it's pacifist furniture.

You'll grow suspicious that the "third bedroom" was once a walk-in closet. There are a lot of mirrors, making the place look twice as large as it really is.

The glossy one-sheet of information on the property will invariably insist it's "stunning." This seems hyperbolic after the first property you've seen, and increasingly ludicrous after each following dozen. If seeing a house or condo that's been cleaned up for an open house left you genuinely *stunned*... you probably couldn't handle the ending twist of an M. Night Shyamalan movie.

"And then we learn he was dead all along!"

(Realtor clutches heart, gasps, dies.)

As you're touring the home, the Stepford Realtor will follow you around, attempting to attach itself to you in a manner similar to the aquatic remora. Like the party guest you just can't seem to ditch, it'll offer one helpful factoid after another, as if you were one bit of trivia away from hocking a kidney on the black market to ensure you could bid over the asking price.

"The kitchen drawer latches are new!"

"The door frames have been completely replaced." (What the heck happened to the old ones? Just what were you doing that generated significant wear and tear on a door frame?)

"The sellers are willing to throw in the ice cube trays with the refrigerator. They're from Restoration Hardware."

"It's got great potential!" *Which means it stinks now.*

Sometimes the home is a rambler, and sometimes the realtor is.

There's only one thing more unreasonable than the expectations of the people who are allegedly trying to sell you their home. That's the expectations of the people who will, a few years down the road, allegedly try to buy your home.

One of the hard lessons of real estate—and life—is that the true value of what you're trying to sell isn't determined by a website, or what other homes have sold for, or recent trends. It's determined by what somebody's willing to pay. Until you've got a buyer who's actually willing to pay, your house is worth 0.

You and your spouse may begin intending to play good cop, bad cop in the negotiations. It's a nice strategy, but you'll eventually find yourself playing bad cop, bad cop, with your realtor assigned the role of the good cop. And then, as negotiations progress, all three of you are going to turn into Dirty Harry, Andy Sipowicz, and Vic Mackey. You will fantasize about smacking the perp/buyer around with a phone book under a hot, sweaty light, demanding answers to questions like, "You thought you could get away with asking for another $3,000 in closing costs covered, didn't you?"

It's just about impossible not to get irked at some point during the sales negotiation process. And by irked I mean driven to a rage that would leave Bruce Banner telling you to see an anger management counselor. It's a perfect formula for stress: enormous sums of money at stake, people's personal attachment to their homes, real and assumed deadlines, and the required approval of banks, loan officers, assessors. I've seen people who were working on high six-figure real estate transactions walk away from deals over differences of $2,000. I suppose it was a bad omen that the buyers were working with the realtor firm of Pennywise and Poundfoolish.

The smaller the disputed point or amount, the more intensely each side will be convinced that the other side should concede it. You thought I was kidding about the ice cube trays earlier. We had a buyer declare that our revised asking price was a bad-luck number, and request a different number. I was tempted to reply, "I hear 8 is a lucky number. Why don't you pay 8 million? Would that be lucky enough for you?" We agreed to reduce the price by a dollar. I was really tempted to ask them to loan me a buck at the closing.

But when it's all said and done, you've completed the deal and are on your way to many happy years in your new home. Just try to ignore the sound of the Darth Vader–like breathing of your bank's mortgage officer.

The Known Unknowns and Unknown Unknowns of Buying a House

Closing on a house is such an odd experience, because it's a blend of terror and banality. There's something truly scary about signing a piece of paper that demands you make sizeable monthly payments to someone for the next thirty years of your life, but you're not just signing one page. No, the process drags on page after page...an initial here, a signature there, and don't forget to date it here, here, and here. I've bought two homes in my life, and both times I just had this awful feeling of "what am I getting into?"

That's partly because the process of buying a house is much more casual than it should be. We try on clothes before we buy them. We can take cars for test drives (I've even had dealers tell me to take a car home for the weekend). But you'll likely spend just a couple of hours in your new home before it is actually yours. Sure, a home inspection will have taken place before you plunk down any money, and it will likely catch most big issues. It's been my experience, however, that even the most conscientious of inspectors won't tell you everything that you'd like to know. You might not even know to ask. The process of buying a house is full of what Donald Rumsfeld called "known unknowns" and "unknown unknowns." You know, for instance, that you don't know and can't tell how effective a home's heating system will be when you're buying a home in July (though you can probably make an educated guess based on how evenly cool the temperature is inside the home with the air-conditioning running). The unknown unknown is something you don't think about, because you don't know to think about it.

The first house we bought was in Oklahoma City. Built in 1912, it was an Arts and Crafts–style house on a huge lot, and it offered slightly more room and a slightly better neighborhood than the rental house we were currently occupying. Even better, it was just a few blocks away so we didn't have to move the kids to a new elementary school. The home passed inspection with a couple of minor issues that were fixed before we moved in, and after undergoing that terrifying process of signing away the next thirty years of my life (or so it felt at the time) the house was ours. So were all of its issues.

The first unknown unknown that popped up was the wiring. Some of it looked like it could have been installed by Edison himself, while other portions looked to be relatively new. I was constantly worried that the old wiring would cause a fire, but we didn't have the money to replace the wiring throughout the house, so it became a "known unknown" that lingered in the back of my mind throughout the rest of the time we owned the house. That worry was compounded when I had to get deep into the crawl space under the house for some unremembered reason and saw that the pillars holding up the house were a mix of cinder blocks and bricks that looked incredibly dangerous and unsteady. To jack up the house and install real pillars would have been thousands of dollars, and we didn't have thousands of dollars to spare. So, for the rest of the time we lived there I would tread as lightly as I could, and I waited at night for the inevitable moment when a brick in the Jenga piles holding up my house would crack and crumble under the weight, causing the entire thing to collapse.

I was really glad to leave that house. But, for what it's worth, it's still standing. The massive oak tree in the backyard is still dangerously (in my opinion) close to the back of the house, towering over the shingled roof and casting its welcoming shade during the blazing summer months. It hasn't burned down and it hasn't collapsed. Maybe I worried over nothing, but when we moved to the D.C. suburbs and sold it, I swore to myself I'd never buy another old home again. There were just too many unknown unknowns.

When we left Oklahoma City, it was one of the most affordable places to buy a home in the country. We moved to the northern Virginia suburbs of Washington, D.C., which was (and is) one of the most expensive places to buy a home. We actually ended up renting the entire time we lived there, which worked out well. There are certainly times when buying a home isn't the responsible, adult thing to do. We liked our neighborhood, but if we bought a home there it would have been right at the cusp of what we could afford, we would have bought a home close to the height of the housing bubble, and we likely would have ended up underwater on our mortgage. We were lucky, but we also recognized that the housing prices were inflated and chose not to buy. "Don't spend what you can't afford" is one of those adages that you don't hear much in Washington, D.C. (or its suburbs), but it's pretty solid advice.

We did eventually buy a home, but it was far from Washington, D.C., and its inflated real estate prices. After months of looking at properties across three states, we found a small farm in central Virginia that actually fit our budget. There's plenty of room for chickens, pigs, goats, a huge garden, our neighbor's cattle in our pasture on occasion, and a safe place for us to go shooting whenever we like. And, despite what I swore to myself, it's old. Really old. The earliest part of the house dates to between 1775 and 1780, and it's been added on to over the years (including a bathroom addition that was done with spectacular incompetence). There've been plenty of unknown unknowns, including an Asian lady beetle infestation, carpenter bees turning my carport into Swiss cheese, a leaky roof, and even running out of the propane that we use to heat our home during a February snowstorm.

Life is full of unknown unknowns, and they shouldn't stop us from buying a home, taking a job in a new city, or any other major life-changing decision. Yeah, it's scary to buy a home, and home ownership comes with a lot of challenges. After renting for years and being reimbursed by my landlord for things like repairs to the home, new appliances, and new flooring, it was definitely an adjustment to have to actually pay for this stuff. Buying a home warranty helped immensely in that respect. (If you buy one, get it from an established home warranty firm. There are a lot of scammers out there with a website and not much else.) We adjusted our budget in a lot of other ways too, and that helped us find our new "normal." And in the meantime, we had something of our own. Something we loved.

You might love a brand-new home that no one's ever lived in before, but that's not really for me anymore. That's the kind of house I grew up in, and while having the latest technology and up-to-date everything is a definite plus, I'd trade it for a house with a couple hundred years of history and the chance to add my own family's memories to the mix. And as it turns out, now that I have my previous experience as the owner of an older home to draw on, I'm not constantly dwelling on what awful things might befall my old farmhouse. When those unknown unknowns pop up, they're more challenges to be conquered, not things to be feared. And when you fix something, having a wife who's as crafty as Martha Stewart and as handy with tools as Nicole Curtis (among a multitude of other talents) really helps.

What Would Ward Cleaver Do?

As a former Navy Seabee, he could *build* a house. Buying a home was probably a comparative breeze for him.

15

Marriage Is for Keeps: How to Avoid Divorce

 When you get married, jump in with both feet. And brace yourself for those hard times, because sooner or later, they'll arrive.

I understand the limited utility of telling a young man, "don't get divorced"; no one sets out on that path deliberately.

There's some good news on this front. The divorce rate is dropping:

The divorce rate peaked at 5.3 divorces per thousand people in 1981, before falling to 4.7 in 1990, and it has since fallen further to 3.6 in 2011, the most recent year for which data are available. Of course, the marriage rate has also fallen over this period. But even measuring divorces relative to the population that could plausibly get divorced—the number of people who are married—shows that divorce peaked in 1979, and has fallen by about 24 percent since.*

I can't help but suspect that many members of Generation X—the generation that grew up with the consequences of nationwide no-fault divorce becoming the law of the land, state by state, from 1970 to 1985— saw the consequences of increasingly common divorce and resolved to avoid that fate for themselves.

In 2013, 191 "Certified Divorce Financial Analysts"—lawyers, accountants, and financial planners who specialize in the financial aspects of divorces—were asked, "According to what your divorcing clients have told you, what is the main reason that most of them are getting (or have gotten) divorced?"

The survey found that** the top reasons were "basic incompatibility" (43 percent), "infidelity" (28 percent), and "money issues" (22 percent). "Emotional and/or physical abuse" lagged far behind (5.8 percent), and "parenting issues/arguments" and "addiction and/or alcoholism issues" received only one half of one percent each.

That term "basic incompatibility" doesn't really illuminate much, does it? Who sets out to marry someone who is "basically incompatible" with them? What happens to make you wake up one morning and conclude you're "basically incompatible" with your spouse?

As I examine the married couples I know, I've concluded that the divorce-triggering "basic incompatibility" must mean something deeper and more significant than fighting. Every couple fights: some rarely, some frequently. Loud fights, angry fights—none of these, by themselves, are indicators that a marriage is in deep trouble.

---

* Justin Wolfers, "How We Know the Divorce Rate Is Falling," *New York Times*, December 3, 2014, http://www.nytimes.com/2014/12/04/upshot/how-we-know-the-divorce-rate-is-falling.html?_r=0.
** "Survey: Certified Divorce Financial Analyst® (CDFA™) Professionals Reveal the Leading Causes of Divorce," Institute for Divorce Financial Analysts™, https://www.institutedfa.com/Leading-Causes-Divorce/.

I do notice that my divorced friends say that fighting rarely resolved an issue. And maybe that was the problem.

There are four ways couples respond to conflict: he concedes, she concedes, they compromise, or it gets swept under the rug.

That last option might be the easiest, but it's a short-term solution at best. Each time you sweep a difficult issue under the metaphorical rug of your day-to-day interaction in your marriage, that rug gets a little harder to walk on. Resentments build. Eventually, the issue you're fighting about stops being the real issue; the real issue becomes your inability to resolve any other issue.

The D-word can actually help a marriage full of conflict. It can be a great clarifier. Using the D-word is the DEFCON Two of marriage. (DEFCON is short for defense readiness condition, the alert state for the U.S. armed forces. DEFCON Five is calmest, DEFCON One is most severe, basically meaning nuclear war is imminent.) When your spouse uses the D-word, it is a screaming alarm klaxon that asks you just how much you care about whatever it is you're fighting about at that moment.

Is it worth divorcing your wife over?

Put that starkly, most of the day-to-day problems in a marriage don't look that bad. If you can back down from that moment, you've endured your marital equivalent of the Cuban Missile Crisis. John F. Kennedy's 1963 point about the basic common links with the Soviets applies to most warring spouses: "We all breathe the same air. We all cherish our children's future. And we are all mortal."

The decline in the divorce rate might reflect broader cultural trends in marital counseling and trial separations. As long as each spouse clearly understands the "rules" of the trial separation, they can do a lot of good in some cases. Absence can make the heart grow fonder; space and time can give perspective on just what the problems in the marriage are.

All of this gets a lot more complicated when kids are involved.

Obviously, it's a lot more difficult to raise your child by yourself than with a loving partner. If you're a single parent, doing the best you can,

God bless ya. The Lord knows—and I know—you're doing the best you can in extremely stressful circumstances.

My only tastes of single parenthood come when my wife is away on business trips or sick. A few years back, she had one particularly nasty bout with bronchitis that left her bedridden, and I can say with pride that I handled all the household duties with our two boys like clockwork for four days. By the fifth day, I was checking on her with new urgency. By days six and seven, standards were slipping—*"Okay, fine! You want cereal for dinner? Go right ahead!" "You don't want to wear a coat? Fine. Go freeze."* By the eighth day, I was pointing out that even God got to rest on His seventh day. Thankfully, by day nine she had recovered.

To take care of every little detail in raising your child or children, day in and day out, with no relief on the horizon, is Herculean.

To quit a marriage because of it is more than a mistake; it's shirking your responsibility. Unfortunately, it's increasingly common in America today. Through a million individual choices, our society is engaging in a giant, high-risk experiment: Just how well can a child grow and develop without a father in the picture? According to the Pew Research Center, in 2014 just 46 percent of American children under the age of eighteen lived in a home with two married heterosexual parents in their first marriage. A generation ago, in 1980, 61 percent of kids grew up in those circumstances. What dramatically expanded in the past two generations were single-parent households: 9 percent in 1960, 19 percent in 1980, 34 percent today.

I can't think of a better definition of a failed man than a deadbeat dad. If you bring a child into the world, your purpose in life is to be involved with that child and guide him to adulthood. Fatherhood is a job you don't get to quit. Fathers teach sons how to be men; they teach daughters what to expect from men.

Maybe a divorce will be an unavoidable chapter in your life's story. If it occurs after you become a dad, you absolutely must dig down deep and try to keep your relationship with your spouse as cordial and respectful as possible, and to keep the focus on your children's best interests.

You may be raging inside, but neither she nor the kids need to see that. Save it for your buddies or your lawyer.

There are amiable divorces, and there are children of divorce who go on to live happy, fulfilled lives. But there's some distinctly disturbing social science research out there.

Psychologist E. Mavis Hetherington is one of the preeminent social scientists researching divorce, and her book, *For Better or for Worse*, was generally seen as indicating that many children of divorce grow up just fine. But take a look at the fine print on those statistics: "Twenty-five percent of youths from divorced families in comparison to 10 percent from non-divorced families did have serious social, emotional, or psychological problems."* One way to look at that statistic is to say that 75 percent of children of divorce will turn out okay. Another way is to say that divorcing parents increase the odds of their children enduring those serious problems from 1 in 10 to 1 in 4.

"Boys raised in a single-parent household were more than twice as likely to be incarcerated, compared with boys raised in an intact, married home, even after controlling for differences in parental income, education, race, and ethnicity."

For girls, "one-third of girls whose fathers left the home before they turned 6 ended up pregnant as teenagers, compared with just 5 percent of girls whose fathers were there throughout their childhood."

There's a considerable public wariness about the increasing rate of single parents, in particular single mothers. In 2011, the Pew Research Center asked Americans how they felt about a variety of social trends,** including more single women having children without a male partner to help raise them. They concluded society was split into three roughly

---

* W. Bradford Wilcox, "The Kids Are Not Really Alright," *Slate*, July 20, 2012, http://www.slate.com/articles/double_x/doublex/2012/07/single_motherhood_worse_for_children_.html.
** Rich Morin, "The Public Renders a Split Verdict on Changes in Family Structure," Pew Research Center, February 26, 2011, http://www.pewsocialtrends.org/2011/02/16/the-public-renders-a-split-verdict-on-changes-in-family-structure/.

equivalent groups, Accepters (31 percent), Rejecters (32 percent), and Skeptics (37 percent).

That categorization feels like a deliberately opaque way of describing public attitudes—along with the headline "The Public Renders a Split Verdict on Changes in Family Structure." "Split" can mean anything. When a sample divides 99 to 1, it's still technically "split."

And for some of these subsamples, that's exactly what they found. Unsurprisingly, 98 percent of the "Rejecters" say "more single women having children without a male partner to help raise them" is a bad thing for society. What you might not expect is that 99 percent of the "Skeptics" feel the same way. So taken as a whole, something in the range of 68 percent of Americans think it's bad that more single women are raising children alone.

Quite a few media outlets, including NPR, construed the poll result as a public expression of condemning single mothers. But the poll question isn't so precise. I'd bet a doughnut that if you sat down with those Rejecters and Skeptics, they would express great sympathy for those single mothers, and contempt or disgust for the absent fathers.

I don't know why the statement "kids need moms and dads"* gets construed as an attack on single parents. I suppose it's a short psychological

---

* You may have noticed this whole book is really, really "heteronormative," as the social justice warriors say. Look, if you're gay or lesbian, I hope you're enjoying this book and I hope life treats you well. I don't doubt gays and lesbians can be fine parents.

But please refrain from whining that a book about parenting and manhood written by two straight guys doesn't spend enough time discussing the gay perspective. Based on data from the 2013 CDC National Health Interview Survey, 96.6 percent of American adults identified as straight, 1.6 percent identified as gay or lesbian, and 0.7 percent identified as bisexual. The remaining 1.1% of adults identified as "something else," stated "I don't know the answer," or refused to provide an answer.

For some reason, Americans walk around believing that gays make up a very large minority in this country. Gallup found in 2015 that "the American public estimates on average that 23% of Americans are gay or lesbian." The mean estimate from respondents ages eighteen to twenty-nine was 28 percent. So let's be clear: when we talk about the "One Percent," we're talking about the super wealthy; when we talk about the "Two Percent," we're talking about homosexuals.

step from "divorce is bad for kids" to "divorced people are bad people," and most people who go through the emotional, psychological, and financial toll of divorce feel like they've been through enough without another serving of societal disapproval. And they're right. It's needlessly cruel to kick them when they're down.

Divorce is a hard road to travel—hard enough to make exploring every alternate route worthwhile.

The Kids Are All Right

You may have noticed that, compared to most of the chapters in this book, Jim's piece on divorce was a little long on data and short on personal anecdotes. That's because, luckily for Jim, he doesn't really have any personal experience with divorce. I, on the other hand, watched my parents get divorced before I was ten years old. I married a woman whose parents were also divorced, and whose first marriage had fallen apart a few years before we met. And over the eighteen years that I've been married (as of this writing), there've been a few times when divorce seemed like it might be in my future as well.

Jim paints a pretty grim picture of the children of divorce: more likely to end up in prison, more likely to end up on a reboot of *Teen Mom*, and simply more likely to end up *messed up* than the product of a two-parent family. Thankfully, I've never been to prison, I've only impregnated my wife, and I consider myself to be fairly well grounded, though I did have my share of adolescent angst when I was younger. Growing up, I had plenty of friends who were being raised by single moms, and they all turned out okay too (at least as of the last high school reunion).

That's not to say my mom wasn't concerned about my mental well-being while she and my dad were going through their divorce. My mother had moved my older brother and me back to Oklahoma, while my father stayed in New Jersey (where we had moved a couple of years prior). She sent us to a seemingly endless series of counselors (I remember three, but there may have been a few more), which I think may have done more harm than good. At the time, while I didn't like the fact that my parents were splitting up, I didn't know what to do other than try to adjust to my new reality. Talking to counselor after counselor about how I "really" felt just made me feel like I was supposed to be taking it harder than I really was. I was upset, but I wasn't devastated. Dad was a salesman who was gone half the time anyway. I missed him, but I grew up missing him. This wasn't really anything new.

Rarely will you hear a therapist tell someone, "Hey, you know what? You're good. I really don't think I can do anything for you." No, in my case I must have been repressing my true feelings about the divorce. And the prime piece of evidence the therapists had was my science grade.

It's pretty hard to fail fourth grade science. If you can spell "earth" and know how to make a dinosaur diorama for the Science Fair, you're pretty much guaranteed passage. Yet for some reason I wasn't turning in my homework for fourth grade science, and when the teacher finally told my mom about halfway through the semester, both my mother and the various counselors were convinced that this meant I was acting out to get attention. It had nothing to do with the divorce, though. It was all about my mom's lunch schedule.

See, one day not long after the semester began, I spaced on doing my homework. The teacher told me to go to the principal's office and call my mom to let her know. I left the classroom, walked through the cafeteria, and into the school office. I told the secretary I needed to call my mom, dreading having to tell her that I was getting a zero on my homework that day. When I called her office, however, the receptionist told me that my mom was at lunch. Did I want to leave a message? Well, I wasn't about to tell this woman to tell my mom that I was in trouble for not doing my homework, so I said, "No thanks," hung up, and walked back to class. The teacher asked if I'd called my mom, I said yes, and that was the end of it.

That Was The End Of It. Nothing else happened. And so I quit doing my homework. I didn't tell my mom, and about every three days my teacher would tell me to go call my mom. I would, I'd never leave a message, and I'd go back to class. Looking back, it's kind of bizarre to me that my teacher didn't reach out to my mom earlier, because this *was* a problem, just not a cry for help. It was more about laziness and short-sighted stupidity.

Anyway, I relate this story because I'm not sure I buy the statistics that try to prove that divorce is going to cause irreparable harm to the kids involved. That's not to say it doesn't suck, but it's also not an excuse to destroy your life if your parents end up splitting. Absolutely none of the parents I know who've gotten divorced say it was because they just had to get away from the kids, so try not to take it personally if it happens.

It's harder not to take it personally when they're not really involved after the divorce, however. As I mentioned, we'd moved back to Oklahoma while my dad was still in New Jersey, so joint custody was a non-issue. I saw my dad when he'd come out to Oklahoma for business, which was about every six months or so. We'd talk on the phone more regularly than that, but our conversations were always pretty brief (even today, it's rare for us to have a phone conversation that lasts longer than ten minutes). The nadir in our relationship came one October, when a package showed up in the mail. Inside was a birthday card and my sixteenth birthday present: a beach towel. My birthday is in August. And seriously, a beach towel for my sixteenth birthday? It's not like I was expecting a new car or anything, but a beach towel?

I actually didn't talk to my dad for a couple of years after that. With the impeccable logic of a hormonal sixteen-year-old, I decided Dad's belated gift must mean he didn't care much about me. That being the case, I was bound and determined not to care much about him. As I grew up, my feelings thawed. One evening during my freshman year of college I picked up the phone and called his house. I almost hung up when he answered, but instead took a drag off my cigarette and said, "Hi, Dad." To his credit, he knew who I was immediately, greeting me by name.* I told him that I was tired of being angry at him and tired of not having

---

* This is a bigger deal than it might seem. My dad was notoriously bad about calling all of us kids by each other's name, or even the names of family pets living and dead. I do the same thing now that I'm grown, but I'm not sure if it's because I have so many kids and pets or this is a weird genetic quirk passed down on the father's side of the family.

my dad in my life. He told me he was sorry for not being as involved as he should have been. It was another short phone call, but it started to repair the damage done.*

Flash forward a few years and I was dealing with another father who was largely absent from the scene. Only this time it wasn't my dad, it was the biological father of my oldest kids. When my wife and her kids moved from New Jersey to Oklahoma, it's not like anyone had any expectations that he would be able to come visit on a regular basis. Still, regular phone calls or letters to the kids would have been nice. When a birthday or a holiday would go by with no contact, I would see the looks of disappointment on the faces of my kids. I'd get so angry that I'd write letters to him that I never sent (eventually we wouldn't even know where to send them). The fact that child support was sporadic (to say the least) didn't bother me. We could take care of our family without his money. What killed me was seeing my kids go from disappointment that they didn't hear from their biological father to the resigned expectation that he was going to let them down again. Eventually, on one rare occasion when he called, my daughter declined to talk to him. The next time he called, my son followed his sister's lead. Their dad never called back.

Always Remember Why You Got Married in the First Place

While my wife's ex was slowly removing himself from the picture, our own marriage hit a serious rough patch. As I said earlier, there've been a couple of occasions when divorce seemed like it was a possibility, and this was the first of those times. There were moments where both of us would have said that the primary reason we were staying together was for the kids. I know I felt like I couldn't let them down. I couldn't walk out on them. If my wife had been childless when we married, we very well might have both walked away at the first real difficult moment.

---

* My father and I have a great relationship now. He's a good man, if somewhat forgetful about birthdays. I love him dearly and am so glad that I grew up enough to get over my fit about feeling unimportant.

Instead, neither one of us was willing to do that to our kids. And it was that recognition that we were both on the same page about our kids that ultimately allowed us to work together to make our marriage stronger.

We decided to see a counselor, and after a couple of sessions we realized that we were actually getting along better. It's not that he was a brilliant mind or anything. Actually, he reminded us of Ned Flanders from *The Simpsons*. We were both highly amused, and we'd get in the car and start talking about him instead of arguing. Maybe laughter really *is* the best medicine. After three weeks of this, we came to some conclusions: We did love each other, and we loved our family. We didn't want the marriage to end. We both needed to make some changes to be more engaged in our marriage, and not just go through the motions of playing our roles of spouse and parent. And that's what we did.

We actually enjoyed a second honeymoon period for a couple of years. Many more years passed where our marriage was strong and stable, if not burning with the white-hot passion of a newly recommitted relationship. Eventually, though, the shared spheres of our lives began to become more separate. Our conversations dwelled on the dull and mundane, our interests were becoming more divergent, and our patience with each other became more strained. A deep chill had set in over our relationship again, without either of us really becoming aware. On some level, despite the problems we were having, we both convinced ourselves that our marriage was just fine. The truth was it had become a zombie marriage shambling along, slowly rotting away but still moving forward.

"Irreconcilable differences" is a pretty vague phrase, but I wonder how many divorces start with this kind of scenario; no huge nasty split but a simple drifting apart. Most people continue to grow as individuals throughout their life, but what happens when we grow apart from someone we love? When do the differences stop being reconcilable and become insurmountable problems?

At the lowest point, the only thing keeping us together was the fact that neither one of us wanted to be the villain leaving the other one. I read a book about the Stoics around the same time, and I adopted the habit of trying to imagine the worst moments about getting divorced, like telling my wife that it was over and that I was giving up. Sitting my children down and telling them I wouldn't be living with them anymore, but that I still loved them. Coming home to a sad, empty apartment. There were dozens of vignettes I would play out in my head. My body would ache inside as I walked myself through each scenario night after sleepless night, but it helped me understand that I didn't want my marriage to end. I wanted my marriage to be better. Thankfully, my wife wanted the same thing, and we once again decided we were going to address the issues in our relationship.

This time around, it wasn't so much a second honeymoon as it was a new chapter. We were older now, and our relationship troubles hadn't taken the form of too many loud and angry arguments, but rather cold looks and frosty silences. When we began working on our troubles, our chilly relationship began to thaw, and in addition to our recommitment (or our re-recommitment, I suppose) there was a sense of renewal to our relationship as well. We weren't interested in simply shoring up our marriage or patching over the problems. We wanted to rebuild a better foundation, and I think we have.

I understand that not all differences are reconcilable, and most of the friends I've had who've gone through a divorce tried very hard to make their marriages work. Both my parents married multiple times, and if it weren't for my wife and her ex splitting up, I would never be the man I am today. I am not here to condemn divorce or people who've gotten a divorce (I generally try to tend to the beam in my own eye before worrying about someone else's mote). All I know is that I'm glad we stuck with it through the hard times. I'm thankful our differences were (and are) not irreconcilable, even if they can still lead to...let's say spirited debate on occasion. I am truly blessed to have my family, to love them and be loved by them, and I'm mindful of this fact every day.

What Would Ward Cleaver Do?

Ward had his priorities straight: he kept his focus on his relationship with June and the kids. Work paid for the mortgage, but a marriage and family is forever.

PART IV
Fatherhood

A father has to be a provider, a teacher, a role model,
but most importantly, a distant authority figure who can
never be pleased. Otherwise, how will children
ever understand the concept of God?

—Stephen Colbert

16

Fatherhood Is Not Something to Be Avoided

 We're big on protecting endangered species in this country. We'll deny water to farmers so that the tiny delta smelt can live on a little longer in the wild. We'll protest the hunting of wolves, but won't shed a tear for the livestock they eat. Similarly, we'd freak out if birthrates started plummeting among animals in our national parks, but we don't even blink when it happens to the birthrates for humans across the nation. Starting in the 1960s the birthrate in the United States dropped dramatically, and we've never really recovered. Now we're starting to see record-low levels in our total fertility rate, particularly among women in their twenties. As of 2012, the TFR was just 1.88 births per woman, down from 3.8 in the 1950s. We've gone through periods of low birthrates before, notably in the 1920s through the early 1940s, but never has the rate been so low for so long.

What's going on? Part of the answer can be found in the smaller number of people in their twenties getting married, but there are also fewer births to single mothers as well. The usual suspects tend to get the blame for our declining birthrate: economic uncertainty because of the Great Recession, greater student loan debt, an extended adolescence compared to previous generations; these are among the more common theories floated by academics and the purveyors of conventional wisdom. It may also be, or so we're told, that those men and women who aren't struggling financially in our moribund economy are too busy leading fabulous lives to want to be tied down with a kid.

Mostly, then, the theories seem to focus on being too afraid to have kids (or too risk-averse if you want to sound nicer). This is perfectly reasonable. I was terrified at the thought of having a baby, and that was after I'd been called "Dad" for three years by my oldest daughter and son.* I kind of felt like I had lucked out and missed all the really hard stuff like midnight feedings, diaper changing, and what I assumed would be hours and hours of crying for no reason at all. Plus, having a baby is expensive! All the diapers, wipes, baby clothes, strollers, high chairs, cribs, and other baby necessities I wasn't even aware I'd be purchasing would be more than our budget could handle. No way, I told my wife when she first brought up having another child. Let's wait a few years.

Well, we didn't wait a couple of years. My son was born about ten months after we had that conversation, actually. My wife told me, with the authority of having had two kids already, that there really wasn't ever a "good" time to have a child, if that meant we were waiting for a big enough balance in our savings account or that perfect moment in our professional lives to introduce a baby into the mix. We were never going to have another child if we waited for the stars to align perfectly. Meanwhile, she was already in her mid-thirties and didn't want to wait too much longer to get pregnant. So, despite some lingering hesitation on my end, we decided to have a kid. I know many parents out there struggle

---

* This gets confusing, I know. I refer to all of my kids as "my kids," even though I'm technically the stepfather to my two oldest kids. I'm Dad, they're my kids, and if you don't like it, that's your problem.

to conceive, and I feel for them, but that wasn't an issue for us. In fact, it happened the first weekend we tried to make a baby. I was actually kind of hoping it would take a little longer, both because it's fun to try and make a baby and the fact that we were still "trying" meant that having a baby was still a theoretical thing. That didn't work out so well, but as it turned out, when I found out we were really going to have a baby I didn't panic. Well, not outwardly, anyway.

Being one of those obnoxious first-time fathers, I documented my wife's pregnancy through my job. At the time, I was still working as a reporter for the local news/talk radio station in Oklahoma City, and I put together a weekly series called "The Daddy Diaries." Each week covered a different aspect of preparing to have a baby, from telling the kids to going to parenting class. I even brought the microphone and recorder into the hospital room, though one look from my wife during her contractions and I smartly put both away until after my son was born.

In a way, putting this out there for the world to hear made me a little braver than I might have been otherwise. I talked myself into thinking that I had put away my fears and uncertainties about becoming a father to an infant, when in reality I still had plenty of insecurities about how I was doing as Dad to my son and daughter. I was twenty-six years old and I was getting ready to be a father of three. The future seemed vaguely terrifying to me. I wasn't sure I was up for this, and I certainly wasn't going to tell my ever-expanding wife that I was worried I was going to fall flat on my face as a father at some point in the not-so-distant future.

If I couldn't talk to the mother of my kids, I could talk to my own mom, and that's exactly what I did. My mom had warmed up to our marriage by then, thankfully. Actually, every one of our parents had come around by that point. They could tell that, as inexplicable as it was for us to have gotten married so quickly, we were in it for the long haul. She was thrilled at the prospect of having another grandchild, so I did take that into account when she told me that I would be a great father. What I wasn't expecting was her confession that she still had doubts about her own ability as a parent.

I know my mom wasn't perfect, just like every other parent out there. My wife thinks that my mom was nuts to give me as much freedom as she did starting from age eleven or twelve, but I think (A) she knew I was pretty responsible for my age, and (B) even if it was kinda bonkers to let a twelve-year-old go to a Journey concert by himself, it really helped me become a more responsible and mature adult. I wasn't interested in drinking or doing drugs at these concerts. I was there to hear the music: Whitesnake, Stryper (yeah…), Bon Jovi, Def Leppard's "Hysteria" tour with Tesla opening. My mom appreciated that I loved music and trusted that I wouldn't take advantage of her not wanting to go to a metal concert.

After I became an adult I realized that my mom had an ulterior motive beyond trying to foster my ability to take care of myself. When I was at a concert, she and her boyfriend could have some alone time. As it turns out, she actually felt a little guilty about dropping me off so she could have a Friday night with her fella. Talking with my mom made me realize that it was okay not to be an expert at parenting. Maybe we never are. Maybe we always second-guess something we said or did, because we're constantly learning how to be a *better* parent, even if we'll never be flawless. As Jim Gaffigan says, "Most of the time I feel entirely unqualified to be a parent. I call these times being awake."

And so came the big day. My wife's due date was around our anniversary, but that day came and went, and so did my birthday the following day. By the fifth day past her due date we were trying all of the standard folk remedies to induce labor: walking up and down the street (in triple-digit temperatures. This was Oklahoma in August, after all), warm baths, awkward and uncomfortable sex. The folk tales don't specify that it *has* to be awkward and uncomfortable, but it inevitably will be. Everything is awkward and uncomfortable when you're nine months pregnant. Nothing worked, so we made an appointment to induce labor.

We showed up at the hospital bright and early. The doctor explained that my wife would be put on an IV drip of a medicine that would induce contractions; within a few hours, she should be in full blown labor; and given that she'd gone through this a couple of times before, the labor should be quick. I noted that she didn't mention painless, but my wife asked about the possibility of having something for the pain when it was appropriate. The doctor agreed, and left us in the hands of the nurses.

Within a few hours my wife was having regular contractions, but she wasn't dilating and our son's arrival seemed no more imminent than it did when we arrived. Throughout the day my wife lay on the bed in her birthing suite, miserable with every contraction and a uterus that was clamped shut like a bear trap. In mid-afternoon the nurses conferred and told us that they were likely going to send us home at 5 p.m. We'd have to come back again in the morning.

My wife swears our son must have heard this, for not two minutes later he did an enormous flip-kick in her womb, breaking her water and jump-starting the labor process. After hours of inaction, all of a sudden all hell was breaking loose in the birthing suite. My wife's uterus had gone from "not really dilated" to "Is the doctor going to make it to the room in time?" in what seemed like an instant. Nurses were flying in and out of the room bringing in all the items necessary to deliver a baby. My wife, meanwhile, was trying to get the attention of one of them long enough to remind them about the anesthesia she'd requested. One of them must have alerted the anesthesiologist, because he walked in shortly afterward and told my wife that he was going to gently jab a big honking needle in her spine in order to pump the painkilling drugs into her body. I might be rephrasing a little. There was a slight risk of paralysis if he didn't do it right, but whatever.

The good news is he did it right. The bad news is it didn't work, as he also warned us might be the case. My wife's right leg became completely numb, but that was about it. She could still feel everything else. And when you give birth to a ten pound five ounce baby with a head circumference of fifteen inches, there's a lot to feel. I did what I could, letting her crush the bones in my hand while she rode out each contraction. She held on until the doctor arrived, but literally no sooner had she positioned herself than she ended up grabbing my son as he popped out kind of like a watermelon seed flicked between two fingers. Oklahoma's produced some pretty good catchers, including Johnny Bench, but he had nothing on our OB-GYN that day.

The nurses whisked my son away to a corner of the room, and I stayed by my wife's side while they administered the APGAR test, weighed him, and cleaned him up. Soon enough they told me I could come over, and I approached my little boy for the first time. I had no fear. None. I was full of wonder and amazement and every synapse of my brain felt like it was firing at once, but I wasn't afraid at all. I looked down at this little tiny Winston Churchill lookalike, and I felt the tears well up in my eyes.

"What does he look like?" my wife asked from the bed.

"He's funny looking, like his dad," I replied with a laugh as I snuffled back my tears. "He's incredible," I added. "He's got blue eyes, and no hair whatsoever. He looks happy. He looks really alert."

The nurses told me it was okay to pick him up, and I reached down and took him in my hands, cradling him gently against my arms. I felt weak in the knees, yet so incredibly strong. I carried him over to his mother, and she beamed when she saw him for the first time. She reached out her arms and nestled him close, and he snuggled in and stared up at her with his deep blue eyes. I left the two of them and ran to pick up our kids from our home, where a friend had been watching them.

The three of us hurried back to the hospital after a quick stop at Sonic at my wife's request (a double cheeseburger and a lime slush can work wonders on the body's ability to recover after giving birth). Our kids were excited to meet their baby brother, but I think they both worried about how their lives would be changing as a result. Having a kid is a big deal for everyone involved, including your other kids (more on that later), and I understood that once again, they were being asked to make another big adjustment in their lives. They both gathered close to their mom, one on either side, and she held them tight until they wriggled away with smiles on their faces.

Because my wife had given birth so late, she was able to stay an extra day, but soon she was being wheeled out to the front door of the hospital, our family a little larger than it was when we'd arrived. The new car seat (a gift from her dad) was installed in the back of my wife's Pontiac Grand Prix, and I handled my son like he was made of glass as I placed him in the seat and buckled him in, checking three or four times to make sure he wasn't being pinched anywhere. I settled in behind the wheel, my wife by my side, and we drove off toward the start of a new chapter in our life.

Fourteen years later that tiny little baby had turned into a handsome young man nearly six feet tall. He leaned against the counter in our kitchen, munching on some blueberries from our bushes, and asked me a question about this book. "Why would you want to have a kid?" he asked. "It just seems like they're a lot of money and aggravation."

I don't know that you can understand when you're fourteen. I don't know that you're *supposed* to understand why you'd want a child if you're a fourteen-year-old boy. So I wasn't quite sure how to explain it. I wasn't even sure I had the words to explain it to an adult.

I took him to the front staircase in our old farmhouse. The wall leading to the second floor is covered with photos of our kids. I pointed one photo out to my son. In it, he and I are walking down the sidewalk in front of our house. He is just learning to walk, and both of his arms are up in the air for balance. I'm right by his side, my hand extended out where he can grab hold if necessary, but giving him the space he needs to try to figure out this walking stuff on his own.

"This is why you have kids. Moments like that one on the wall, and even moments like this one right now. That picture is better because you're in it. My life is better because you're in it. And maybe one day you'll feel the same way about a child of your own," I told him. He didn't look convinced.

"There is another reason to have a kid," I mused.

"What's that?"

"Free labor! Come help me mow the yard."

He rolled his eyes and smiled, and the two of us headed outside into the sunshine, walking together down the path to the shed where we store our lawnmowers. The sight would have made for a great picture to complement the one on the wall, but I've got the memory instead, along with a million other moments with all five of my kids that make me so grateful and thankful that I'm their dad.

Jim

So You Are Having a Baby: Pregnancy

Congratulations! Your wife has peed on a stick, and it turned blue.

You're probably eager to tell the world. There are some who say you shouldn't announce a pregnancy for the first three months; the risk of miscarriage drops after that first trimester. It's completely understandable that couples who are thrilled at the news share it a bit early. And it's completely understandable that you, as a man, are itching to share this good news. "We're expecting" has that wonderful "I am a virile, fertile man" subtext. Like Walt Whitman, you contain multitudes.

The problem with waiting for three months is that you have to act "normal" for about twelve weeks. And your life, quite quickly, will become anything but normal. Your wife, who previously ate like a bird, will begin out-eating you. She will cry during Meineke commercials. And obviously, she won't be able to drink. Now, you may be thinking, "Wonderful, no more bickering over who's the designated driver for the next few months," but your wife's social circle knows her. They'll notice if she's having a juice or soda instead of her usual Cosmopolitan or red wine. Maybe ordering tonic water instead of a gin and tonic will fool them for a while, but a lot of women turn into Sherlock Holmes when it comes to each others' possible pregnancies. They'll notice any faint signs of weight gain. They know what your wife's normal appetite is, and— wait, I'd swear there was a whole pizza JUST HERE. She could not have eaten it that fast.

Your lives have been turned topsy-turvy, with all kinds of unexpected twists. Remember all of that deliberately scheduled, fervently procreative sex you were having during ovulation periods? It's not like you ever didn't like it—sex, like pizza, is still pretty good even when it's bad—but you thought pregnancy would slow things down a little. Ha-ha, surprise, without warning your wife's sex drive has been turned up to eleven! And then, just when you think it can't get any better, your wife will be hit by morning sickness.

Yes, your wife will be aglow during this time. Maybe it's radiation.

The snow globe of your life has been picked up and vigorously shaken, and you're expected to hide all of this from everyone except your family and closest friends. When you do finally end the charade, you'll learn your female friends will have suspected from early on. Your male friends will have been completely oblivious.

Your male hormones will go haywire as well. When my wife was pregnant with our first child, she noticed that one weekend afternoon I was getting choked up—*verklempt*, as they say in Yiddish. She asked what it was and the only answer I would give was, "I just want to see him so much!" It was half-magical, half-irritating that my entire life was turning upside down, and I was assembling cribs and changing tables and our house was filling up with unbelievably tiny onesies and diaper genies and yet my only glimpse of him was a profile shot from the ultrasound.

Our second pregnancy—yes, I know there's some debate as to whether that's the appropriate pronoun—had some challenging moments, although thankfully everything turned out fine. Mere moments after being informed we would have another boy, the doctor expressed some concern about one of his measurements, and said that it indicated a higher risk of serious complications, particularly when coupled with what my wife's age would be at the delivery date. Apparently on one side of the birthday, the formula indicates everything will be fine; on the other side of the birthday, the formula indicates that there's a 50-50 chance my wife will give birth to an alien lizard baby from *V*. (It didn't help that the doctor looked like Frank Gorshin playing the Riddler on the old *Batman* television series. "*Riddle me this, Mr. Geraghty! What has three hands, currently swims, but someday will fly with bat wings? Your next offspring, bwha-ha-ha-ha-ha!*")

Ever the optimist—and a pundit on television, meaning I'm convinced I know everything—I pointed out that he was rounding up my wife's age, which meant that the odds couldn't quite be so dire. He stood his ground in a manner I'm sure he meant to be reassuring but was again, Riddler-esque, walking me through the factors in the risk formula. Nightmare upon nightmare: I'm getting the worst news imaginable, and now I have to do math, too.

She and I stumbled when we told our families, and I'll never forget how I nearly choked on the words every time I had to say them: *"We don't know if he's going to be okay."* I could go through the biological details, but the bottom line was the same. Life had given us a glimpse of a second son through another beautifully ghostly ultrasound profile shot—and then put a metaphorical gun to his head.

For a short while, my beloved and I lived with an uncertainty about our child, and in public tried to act as if everything was normal. As usual, she handled it all better than I did. Suddenly I was the one crying during car repair commercials. I'd be watching a football game at a bar, getting a bit of recommended downtime, and not really focusing on anything because I was paralyzed by the open question of whether my new little guy was going to be okay. WOOMP—out come the tears. I'm sure some patrons thought that I was really exceptionally distressed by the Jets' woeful defense that year.

A few weeks later, we did an additional series of tests; the new tests indicated everything was going fine. F. J. Raymond once said, "Next to being shot at and missed, nothing is really quite as satisfying as an income tax refund." That second pregnancy was my near-miss with an event that, had it gone differently, would have broken me. The Man Upstairs has been better to me than I ever deserved.

But life's worst moments are good for something; they put everything else in perspective. Bad day at work? Big fight with my wife? Traffic? *Psshht.* Nothing. Man, you can bring the Hell's Angels, IRS auditors, ISIS, the Bloods and the Crips, a herd of velociraptors, and the Black Hole Oakland Raider fans to my door and I'll rumble with the whole crowd, because it's still easier than hearing the words, *"We don't know if your child is going to make it."*

Pregnancy Step Two: Lamaze

Go to Lamaze class if your OB-GYN recommends it. It can't hurt.

This is not to say you'll find it to be the most edifying class you'll ever take. Lamaze classes are mostly useful for encountering other couples that you are glad you will never see again. Really, there's nothing like watching another man's wife, who appears to be shoplifting a basketball, who's overheated and irritated, and who's decided to take out all of her frustration upon him, lamenting loudly how the air-conditioning in his car isn't working right, and she's been telling him to take it in to fix it, and why didn't he take it in knowing that the hottest summer months were coming, and can we turn the air-conditioning up in this room, and—and basically, everyone else in the class is convinced she's carrying Damien. It only took one look at that woman for me to turn to my wife and tell her how much I love her...and I really love that she's not that woman.

I'd like to think my wife was equally appreciative that she wasn't married to the guy in Lamaze class who was *extremely eager* to participate in the birthing process, and kept joking that he was his wife's "coach." Sure, pal. When your wife is going through contractions that can be measured on the Richter Scale, I'm sure she'll feel endlessly reassured that you've decreed yourself to be her Mike Ditka.

The class was fine, if a little lengthy, and it felt a little silly to be sitting on the mats on the floor pretending to breathe rhythmically, knowing in the back of our heads that the real thing would feel nothing like this. It's a bit like those instructions from the flight attendant right before takeoff. Sure, it all sounds good, proceeding from step to step in the abstract, but when it hits the fan and the plane is in a nosedive, how many of us are really going to remember to fix our own oxygen masks before assisting those around us?

Our Lamaze teacher really seemed to think everyone in the class would all bond over this, like we would all become Lamaze drinking buddies...getting together for day trips to other hospitals...maybe joining the National Lamaze League and getting together to watch the

Lamaze Bowl. Ma'am, I'm sorry, but the only thing we have in common is that we all had phenomenal intimate times around last Christmas.

During the inevitable "does anyone have any questions?" segment, one couple in our Lamaze class asked a question about circumcision with the very clear subtext, "WE HAVE BEEN FIGHTING ABOUT THE TOPIC OF CIRCUMCISION CONSTANTLY. PLEASE TELL MY SPOUSE THAT HIS/HER OPINION IS WRONG."

Pregnancy Step Three: Delivery

We've all heard Bill Cosby's stand-up routine about his wife enduring contractions in the delivery room, standing up in the stirrups, and grabbing him and demanding morphine and bellowing with rage, "YOU DID THIS TO ME!" With that, and every other beleaguered-husband horror story floating through my head, I was braced for the worst. As Jack Davenport declares on the BBC comedy *Coupling*, "There are just some places you don't expect to see a face."

Some people who meet my wife get the wrong impression of her at first. I assure them that underneath her exterior of relentlessly driven, unremittingly determined, cold, steely willpower, she has a hidden core of even more relentlessly driven, unremittingly determined, cold, steely willpower. I used to be jealous when other men would flirt with her. Now I chuckle knowingly and conclude, "Oh, she would break him."

Nonetheless, after hearing all the stories of moms-to-be appearing to be demonically possessed during the birthing process, I was ready for her to cry, to scream, to say nasty things about me, and/or to declare she wasn't going to push him out any further; our son could live there inside of her for the rest of his life. Just build a little womb condo up in there.

Nope. My wife is friggin' bulletproof. The pain of childbirth looked my wife in the eye...and flinched.

Oh, sure, it *hurt*, but when the doctor said, "Push!" she pushed. She bit down and just dealt with what I am sure is the sort of pain that would probably cause my body to not just break but molecularly disassemble. I felt a little better about all the times I had lost an argument to her in that moment, because if childbirth had run up against her and turned tail in defeat, like a giant, neurological Persian army from *300*, then there was no shame in my losing an argument or two.

Sometimes, you'll see newborn babies with coneheads. This is not because they are secretly the offspring of Dan Aykroyd; it is because the baby shifts position inside the womb early, and their head is pointing down, and their head grows in the shape of the bottom of the womb. Babies' skulls are more flexible and aren't like ours, so there's no need to worry, although it looks a little odd. My older son, an unbelievably adorable child, had one of these coneheads when he was born.

The conehead also generated this awkward exchange during those first moments of our son's life:

Her: [grimacing] Can you see it?
Me: I can see the top of the head! You're doing great!
[Pushing]
Her: How about now?
Me: I can see the head! Keep it up! You're doing great!
[More pushing]
Her: How about now?
Me: Uh…still the head! Keep going!
[More groaning and pushing]
Me: Um…still more head!
[Even more pushing]
Her: Now?
Me: You're almost done with the head!

The good news is that once you get those shoulders out, it's like a piñata down there—everything else spills out at once.

And then my wife and I got to see perhaps the most joyful sight of our lives, our baby boy. Of course, throughout this happy moment, I kept thinking of the planet Remulak and the need to "consume mass quantities" and "parental units."

What Would Ward Cleaver Do?

Ward was all about being a dad, so he would have no qualms about the natural consequence of marriage: fatherhood.

∙‖‖|MAN TIPS‖‖|∙

The Fertility Goddess Belly Rub

We really need a national dialogue on touching pregnant strangers. When did this become okay? When did this become expected? She's a mom-to-be, not a petting zoo. Look, all-too-curious person, I don't know where that hand has been. Under what other circumstances does half our society feel the need to touch strangers' bodies? *"Man, that's a heck of a surgical scar, can I feel it?" "Wow, those are some spectacular implants, mind if I take a grope? Ooh, I can feel the silicone kicking!"*

If you find yourself with this compulsion, at the very least have the common decency to ask permission first. In a perfect example of Americans' current drive to apply the law to everything, in 2013, a Pennsylvania man was charged with harassment for allegedly hugging a pregnant woman and rubbing her stomach without her consent.*

If your wife gets a little more clingy during the pregnancy, it may be because her midsection has suddenly become the Golden Idol of Fertility for a society full of Hovitos. Some women report that they get fewer requests for the impromptu public belly button shiatsu when their husbands are around.

And on the flip side, once in a great while you'll encounter a pregnant woman who wants other people to feel her stomach. No, that's okay, ma'am, I take you at your word that you're pregnant. I don't need tactile confirmation. No, thank you, I'm sure your child in there is wonderful, and I'm sure his kicking indicates he'll lead Team USA to the World Cup in about twenty years.

---

* Daniella Silva, "Pennsylvania Man Charged with Harassment for Rubbing Pregnant Woman's Stomach: Cops," NBC News, October 28, 2013.

17

The Greatness of Being a Dad

When you announce that you're expecting, you'll find your friends will give you parenting books. Other than the ones covering the basics—*What to Expect When You're Expecting* and its ilk—most of them are awful. The fatherhood ones are worse than the ones aimed at mothers, and the allegedly funny books on fatherhood usually warrant some sort of literary war crimes tribunal. The cover usually shows the guy with spit-up on his shirt, the diaper falling off the kid, hair messed up, unshaven, bags under his eyes so big they wouldn't fit in an overhead luggage bin, and the author looking out with a stunned, horrified, shocked look on his face. The title is some insufferable variation of, *Oh, God, What Have I Gotten Myself Into? Survival Tips for New Dads Drowning in Their Own Incompetence*, and the whole project sounds like it's designed to make you want to leave the kid on a church doorstep.

Screw that guy on the cover. He's an embarrassment to the rest of us. You are not going to be that guy. Do you hear us? *You are not going to be that guy.* You can handle this. You can rise to the occasion. You are not going to whine about how hard it is.

We wonder if what's intended as comedic exaggeration is seen as reality by fatherhood-averse men. They think, "Oh, I don't want to become that guy!" and think of parenthood as an eighteen-year prison sentence. There are some indicators that society at large is buying into this stereotype of the hapless, bumbling, perpetually overwhelmed dad. The late Stuart Scott observed in his memoir, *Every Day I Fight*:

> I was proud to travel with my kid. I had it down to a science. I wasn't fumbling around like some amateur. I packed a bag; I had the carrier; I'd take the bottles out on the plane and ask the attendant to put them on ice for the flight. It was like clockwork.
>
> Still, people had a hard time wrapping their heads around the sight of the two of us, and it ticked me off. Whether we were in the security line at the airport, boarding a plane, or checking into a hotel, someone would inevitably say, "Oh, look. Mr. Mom." People were trying to be nice—complimentary even. But I hated that. I'm not Mr. Mom. I'm Dad. Is Mom ever Mrs. Dad?
>
> Or how about this one? "Oh, that's so sweet. Dad's babysitting." Seriously? Babysitters get paid. I'm no babysitter. I'm Dad. That sense of surprise, that inability to process the fact of a dad who was as conscientious as a mom—it's a sad commentary on what our culture expects from fathers.[*]

Once you get the hang of it—and you're forced to get the hang of it extremely quickly by circumstances—you can carry yourself with warranted pride.

---

[*] Stuart Scott, with Larry Platt, *Every Day I Fight* (New York: Blue Rider Press, 2015).

A couple months after I became a father, I went to a New Year's Eve party. Our little guy was at that delightful stage where he slept in a carrier for unbelievably long stretches. The Mrs. and I could go out to a restaurant or even a semi-noisy bar and have a nice meal and he would sleep through it, or at least most of it.

At this party, I ended up sitting in a circle of male friends-of-friends. It was one of those odd social circumstances where we're all sitting around, acting like we're all friends, but I didn't actually know any of these guys that well. They all knew each other quite well, at least well enough to bust each other's chops. I was the outside observer—Nick Carraway, peering in at a different social order.

At some point, one of the guys starts busting another guy's chops about being insufficiently manly. I can't remember the precise criteria for the accusation of wimpiness or lameness, but I distinctly remember the accuser, a bit of a loudmouth, was not a father and the guy being accused of it was, like me, a new dad.

(Have I mentioned alcohol was involved? Or is that a given?)

The "turn in your man card" routine went on a little longer than it needed to, at least two jokes past the point of being funny, and I either sympathized with the victim of the mockery, or wanted to knock the teaser down a peg or two—oh, who am I kidding, it was both, and I'm not exactly a shrinking violet in any circumstance.

After yet another "Dude, your testicles have been moved to a safety deposit box" joke from the Don Rickles wannabe, I just stood beside the new dad, pointed at him, and asked, "How many people have you created?"

He chuckled and said, "One."

I turned to the party bully. "And how many human beings have you created?"

He chuckled and saw where I was going with it.

"I think that resolves the 'who's the man' issue."

Dads deal with things, man.

There's fear. Maybe a tougher fear to face than skydivers or surfers or any of the other adrenaline-seeking *Point Break* wannabes face. If you go riding on a motorcycle and wipe out, you're putting your own life at risk. You have some element of control, an ability to assess the risks for yourselves.

With a child, suddenly there's this extremely tiny, extremely vulnerable creature in your life that you love more than yourself, and you cannot ensure your baby's safety with 100 percent certainty. Odds are, everything's going to be fine with your baby, all the way through adulthood. But you can never be certain. What's lurking in their DNA? What germs float through the air? What if some drunk driver is on the same road as you at the wrong time? What if there's a terrorist attack or natural disaster? Kidnappers! (These are exceptionally rare.)

I find myself almost incapable of watching movies or television shows with children in danger now. It's involuntary—my mind Photoshops the faces of my boys onto the screen whenever the adorable moppet is endangered by kidnappers, terrorists, raptors, or kidnapping terrorist raptors.

This doesn't mean a parent's life is consumed by fear; if it is, you're doing something wrong. But to be a parent means accepting a certain amount of powerlessness over fate, a willingness to charge forward in life, even with the risks.

Dads don't get to flinch when it gets gross. When Oprah asked Brad Pitt how fatherhood had changed him, he said, "[I'm] tough as nails. I'm impervious to poo, snot, urine, vomit. You can't get me. You cannot break me down."

Whatever squeamishness a guy has about bodily fluids, he gets over it really fast once a baby enters his life. And it's not some magic Neo-Sees-the-Matrix-Code moment of inspiration. It's just that one moment, "poo, snot, urine, vomit" is coming out with high velocity on the changing table—thankfully, very rarely all at once—and you're the only hazmat team available. You just have to do it. So you do it. There is no motivator more powerful than necessity.

This is not to say fatherhood is easy. Some days it's going to be really, really difficult.

There's a big difference between the hard struggles of parenthood and the hard struggles of any other aspect of life.

To understand why, ask yourself, what do you do all day? What do you make? Reports? Budgets? Car Parts? Buildings?

Maybe you're phenomenally successful, and you can point to recognized triumphs, praise, and respect of your peers. Maybe you're less certain about what all your life's work generated beyond paychecks. At some point in your life, you're going to wonder if all your efforts have paid off. You're going to start asking just how much you do that makes a difference, and whether anything you do will really last. You'll start to think about a legacy.

There is no better, bigger, or more consequential legacy than your child.

It's trite but true that no one, on his deathbed, ever wished he spent more time at the office. I have yet to ever hear a dad say, "You know, that time we went out and kicked the soccer ball around in the yard was an absolute waste of time. We got nothing done, and Junior still can't bend it like Beckham." Yes, kids ask a lot of you—time, energy, sacrifice, patience, care—but ultimately, they're the ones who deserve it most. I know an overworked, quite successful lawyer who became a full-time mom because she got tired of working to the point of exhaustion for obnoxious, ingrate clients. If you're going to be exhausted, be exhausted for the ones who matter most.

The working world may give you a lot, but it very rarely gives you love. Kids have so much love to give, it will stun you.

An aspect of parenting that doesn't get discussed much is the way it can really make you feel empowered.

There is very little in life you get to control. Our daily routines remind us of our powerlessness morning, noon, and night: you awaken to the bad weather, glance at the depressing headlines on the morning news, get stuck in traffic on your morning commute, wonder how serious the rattling noise under the hood is, go to work to grapple with the ever-changing demands of the boss, clients, or customers, spill ketchup on your shirt, fail to get the pretty secretary to smile back at you, realize you have to file your taxes and your in-laws are coming to visit for the weekend.

You get knocked around by the stormy seas of life everywhere else, but when it comes to your children, you're a king. You and your spouse are the two most powerful and influential figures in your child's life. You're more powerful than the rest of the family. You're more powerful than the teachers. You're even more powerful than television. Not even Elmo can overrule your vetoes.

You are now *The Man.* You make the rules, and you get to decide when a rule can be broken. You decide the lessons, and you get to teach them everything you wish you had known when you were little. You get to introduce fresh eyes and ears to everything beautiful and amazing in this world. No matter how the rest of the world sees you, in your child's eyes, you're a giant, and it's not just because they're smaller than you.

For a while, at least—your child will be convinced you know everything. Your ability to do routine tasks—drive a car, climb a ladder, lock a door, hard-boil an egg—will amaze and fascinate them.

Once they get past the stage of messy substances spontaneously ejecting from all orifices, you'll be fascinated with them, too. On meet the teachers night, you'll note that all the other kids' crayon creations are scribbles, but you will marvel at how your child made the sunlight lines emanate so straightly from the yellow spot in the corner. You will really feel like it's one of the most amazing pieces of art you've ever seen, and you will want to save it forever. I know it sounds silly, but it's true. Because it's your kid, and not too long ago, that was just a sleepy, bald, alien-like creature with messy substances spontaneously ejecting from all orifices.

Children are the great clarifier. You may have noticed that some of your peers can become wrapped up in inconsequential aspects of life. They have "drama." They obsess over petty grudges or perceived slights.

Dads ain't got time for that.

Yes, kids will blow up the schedule and rhythm of your pre-parenthood life. They'll wipe away a giant chunk of the time spent on your frivolous enjoyments—your Fantasy Football team, your hours of fiddling around on the Internet, your binge-watching of premium cable television series, your ability to catch a movie at midnight or join the opening-night crowds. But they also wipe away a lot of the inconsequential crap, too. That social engagement you didn't want to attend, but needed an excuse? "I think the baby might be coming down with something." You can tune out that boring conversation; if you're called out on it, you can say, "Oh, I was just thinking about whether we need to renew the baby's prescriptions." That after-work happy hour you just don't want to deal with? Sorry, you've got to pick up your child from day care.

We live in a world where you're expected to multitask. You're expected to perform the roles of husband, employee or breadwinner, son, brother, friend, neighbor, and, when the time comes, father. You're also supposed to take care of your health, to be an informed citizen, to recycle, to avoid micro-aggressions, to reduce your carbon emissions and live sustainably, to file your taxes, to be well-read and cultured.... It's understandable if some days you feel like everybody wants a piece of you, that everybody expects more.

To look upon your infant child is a great clarifier. Clear the decks. Make way. Now you know what comes first. Yes, all of these other people in your life are important. But the vast majority of them will understand when you say, "I have to take care of my child now."

Part of parenthood is watching your childhood memories reenacted live in front of you, from a different camera angle. You will see certain aspects of yourself coming alive in this new person. Then you'll see the parts you're absolutely certain came from your wife. ("My, what a fascinating word you just uttered, Son. Does Mommy say that word when she's driving?") Then you'll see qualities that seem to come from somewhere else.

This is the problem with the modern parenting culture. Everybody feels so obligated to warn you how tough it's going to be, that nobody remembers to tell you how great it's going to be.

Children and the Beautiful Selective Memory of a Father's Frazzled Mind

When you have a small child, a surprising number of strangers will come up to you, inquire about the child's age, and say, "Oh, what a wonderful age!" So far, year after year, I haven't encountered the response, "Oh, that's an awful age. I'm so sorry." Maybe it will happen with teenagers.

Most of the time, I graciously interact with these well-meaning strangers, who are usually parents of children who are now grown. Occasionally, if the boys have been misbehaving, I'll respond, "These children are for sale if you want them."

But as my sons age, I'm beginning to understand the phenomenon.

Our baby days are over; God has been good to us. As I look at pictures of my sons in their baby days, and don't think of the times the poop escaped the diaper, or the frantic repeating of the five S steps—swaddle, side or stomach, shushing,* swinging, and sucking—in an effort to cease a seemingly endless bout of crying, or the days the diaper genie bag broke, or those months where I was so used to wearing a burp cloth over my shoulder I nearly headed into the office with one. (I guess you never know when a coworker might need to burped.)

The human mind is fascinating and mysterious. I know all of those hard times happened, but it takes effort to remember them. My memory needs to be jogged, and it hates jogging almost as much as the rest of me. But the good memories are right there, front and center. My older son's fascination with fall foliage on one of his first walks. Taking him to his first movie, *Toy Story 3*; his rapturous enjoyment; and how he *almost* made it to the bathroom on the way out. His bizarre habit of collecting sticks on every walk, and the need to leave them in a pile outside the front door. When my sons first met, my older son observed:

He: He doesn't talk.
Me: That's right. Babies don't talk until later in life.

---

* Shush the baby, not your wife.

[He studies his newborn brother some more.]

He: He doesn't eat sushi.

Me: Yes, that's true, too.

When I'm describing my younger son to someone who hasn't met him, the first words are his boundless energy and what can only be described as a lust for life. His monkey-like climbing abilities and utter comfort with heights that unnerve his father. His current fearlessness every time we encounter a spider in the house. His inexplicable athleticism that had him lowering his shoulder and tackling and toppling boys twice his size. I'm raising a little Thor.

The past is strange, because we can see it in our mind's eye so clearly, but we know it's gone. It feels like we should be able to go back to a time as easily as we return to a place—psychologically, it's just around the corner. Ultimately, almost everything we do in our daily life passes; only a few iconic moments get preserved. Our old photo albums mostly sit on shelves, collecting dust. Our shakily shot home movies reside on VHS tapes and other formats that we're not even sure we could find a machine to play today. More recent images and snippets of video, constantly descending deeper down into our Facebook archives, a drill marking the passage of time. It would be unbearably sad if, after a long life, this was all that we have left.

But we don't. When we end our ride on this orbiting blue sphere, we parents leave children—half you, half your loved one, and in many cases, capable of amazing things you never could do.

Children aren't a burden. They're a gift.

You're a Parent: Enjoy It

So, what could possibly be so great about caring for every facet of another human being's life for at least eighteen years, which includes being peed on, being subjected to temper tantrums, being told you know absolutely nothing about anything (by your teenagers), watching your kids make mistakes you can't correct, and a thousand other indignities and tribulations?

All of it. Every last moment.

I became a dad of two when I got married at age twenty-three. I had my first biological child by the time I was twenty-six. A few years later I'd become a dad once more, this time to twins. If I said that all of these transitions were easy, it would be a lie of "If you like your plan, you can keep your plan" proportions. In all honesty, I had no clue what I was doing. Yes, you learn from every child, but you also learn that every one of your kids is different, so you're always being kept on your toes.

Thankfully, I had a wise sensei in the form of my wife, who was pretty patient with me. I also started with two wonderful kids who accepted me as "Dad" even if I wasn't their biological father. When you're trying to be a good parent, it helps to have good kids.

Being a parent means never sitting in silence on a train or in a car. It means whipping out your smartphone to answer the sixteenth question starting with "Why" in a ten-minute span. It's introducing someone that's a part of you to the things you love, and sharing the joy of discovery through another set of eyes.

Having a child doesn't make you grow up, unfortunately, but being a parent does. At the same time, it also helps to keep you young. I'm still conversant in the language of video games, despite the fact that I put down the XBox controller (for the most part) a few years ago. An unintended benefit of the Cult of Adolescence is that youth culture, in the form of video games, movies, music, websites, apps, or even the occasional book, is much more approachable to parents than it was in the past. An unintended downside to that, of course, is the growing number of middle-aged women squeezed into pants that read "JUICY" across their rear ends waddling through our shopping malls, but I digress.

We are not only awash in a culture of juvenilia, we're a society of short attention spans, and parenthood is a long game. The goal isn't to make sure your kid can call each day "the best day ever!" It's to make sure your kid turns into a grown-up who can make the world a little bit better. When you realize that, parenting becomes a lot less stressful and a lot more rewarding. I imagine childhood becomes a lot less stressful too. It's not that life magically becomes a Disney Channel sitcom where any family tensions are resolved through a series of wacky (and predictable) events and everything's back to normal in a half hour. There will be times where your kids will drive you crazy. There will also be times where you'll drive them crazy, and the two may not always overlap. But there will also be simple walks in the woods and bedtime conversations that become memories lasting a lifetime. Stupid jokes told at the dinner table will become part of family lore until only the punchline is needed to get your family laughing. A thousand shared experiences will shape who your children are, but they'll also shape you as well. Parenting isn't about checking off a list of daily achievements and scheduled activities. It's a state of being and a way of life. And in my experience, it's a good one.

What Would Ward Cleaver Do?

Of course he'd enjoy being a father; he's the plumb line by which fathers are measured.

18

Your Role in the Mommy Wars

 As a husband and dad, you're going to face the complicated challenge of balancing work and family. At some point early in your parenthood adventure, if the family finances can handle it, you and your wife may contemplate whether you want one of you to stay home and take care of the new baby or little tykes.

You may have strong opinions on whether you want your wife to work outside the home or to be a stay-at-home mom. Ideally, you and your wife can talk honestly about this. If you're going to try to persuade her, and you want to avoid the need to dodge hurled objects from a woman who has probably not had a good night's sleep in several months to a year, you had better start with, "I trust you to make the right decision on this, but I feel strongly that...."

As a husband, you've got two jobs in this situation. The first is to try to help your wife find the option that works best for her and the family as a whole. The second job is to nod sympathetically when she encounters other women who will trigger volcanic rage by implicitly or explicitly criticizing her decisions.

And believe me, they will. For some reason, the discussion about mothers who work and mothers who stay at home hits every mom's sensitive nerve with metronomic regularity. Have you witnessed women fighting on Facebook over working moms versus stay-at-home moms? It makes WWE look like William F. Buckley's *Firing Line*. Ye gods, what a nasty, vicious, raging ideological war! The passive-aggressive denunciations get so furious that both Sunni and Shia clerics are telling them, "Whoa, whoa, whoa, ladies, calm down. Everybody step back a bit. This is really escalating out of control."

This is a deep-rooted, passionate, merciless fight that is not easily understood by outsiders. Kind of like the Balkans. For some reason, when a woman writes, "I made choice A," every woman who made choice B sees the words, "You're not as good a mother as I am." Maybe there's something wrong with Facebook's site, and it's mixed up with Google Translate.

Maybe the easily triggered passions about this issue reveal the extraordinarily difficult pressures women put on themselves. They want to be good mothers, and they want to have thriving, successful, fulfilling careers as well. What's more, they want other people to think of them as being good mothers and thriving, fulfilled professionals, too. They may think that making either choice will be interpreted as a concession on one front. Work, and you're insufficiently devoted to your kids. Stay at home, and you're admitting you just couldn't make it in the working world.

Whether or not any of your wife's friends, siblings, neighbors, and coworkers actually feel that way, there's a good chance your wife will sense somebody, somewhere is disapproving of the choices she's made. Silent judgment is hard to disprove.

Women will accuse us men of being irrational and hot-tempered, but we get upset over really important things, like Fantasy Football, which beer to bring to the barbeque, and whether the guy in front of us used a turn signal.

In a better world, there would be a universal recognition that being a working mom is one of the hardest roles anyone can step into today. (A close second: a working dad.) Everyone would understand that different families will find different arrangements that work best for them. And everyone would understand that working parents get up every morning, do the best they can, and will inevitably make mistakes. The missed PTA meeting, Junior's trip to the principal's office, the embarrassing public tantrum—these reflect momentary and fixable problems on the home front, not an indictment of a parent's choice.

Unfortunately, we don't live in that better, more understanding world, and we probably never will. You can't control all of that; the only thing you can control is yourself, and what you do when some friend of your wife responds with a disbelieving "oh" to her post-birth plans.

You want to support your wife from a quiet, perhaps obscured background location. You're her sniper. Feed her the appropriate social science research and anecdotal evidence indicating that kids raised in the way she chose turn out fine. Whatever you do, you don't want to get directly involved in these fights. These discussions have more landmines than the demilitarized zone between North and South Korea, and as a man, many women will conclude that your Y chromosome makes it impossible for you to understand anything about this issue.

I will say, however, that even though there aren't a lot of them, a lot less heat gets generated over stay-at-home dads. You don't see stay-at-home dads accusing working dads of being bad fathers. And I haven't encountered any working dads who denounce stay-at-home dads who ditch the rat race and devote themselves to taking care of their kids; they never say they're wasting their lives and educations.

Here's our dirty little secret: *we don't really care what other guys do.* Half the time, we're not even listening.

I realize there's a good chance that just offering this opinion will get something thrown at me, but maybe a strategic lack of interest in other people's lives would serve us all well.

What Would Ward Cleaver Do?

Well, Ward didn't have to do anything; it was June who made the "choice" to stay at home, as most moms did in those days. But if Ward were alive today, he'd know the wisdom of staying mum on whatever Mom decided to do.

Don't Outsource Parenting

Over the course of our five kids, my wife has been a college student, a working mom, a stay-at-home mom, and a work-from-home mom. I've always worked, but during the course of our marriage my work schedule has varied from going to work at 4 a.m. to ending my workday at midnight. For most people it's less about making choices about if you're going to stay home or how many hours you're going to work than just doing the best you can in the circumstances you're given. We're lucky in that we've finally reached what for us is the ideal setup. My wife is able to telecommute, and I work nearby, which means we can both attend school functions and help out with doctor's and dentist's visits. But I know not many people can do what we do.

There's some evidence, in fact, that big corporations are pulling back from telecommuting.* The decline in birthrates, especially among Millennials, means companies don't have to be as family-friendly as they did a generation ago. Some of the big corporate campuses seem designed to keep you at your job as long as possible with services and amenities like dry cleaning, doctor's offices, and food courts (as well as day care, it should be noted) offered on site.

And, maybe not surprising, just as some corporations offer on-site day care, the state is eager to step in too, from pushing to lower the age your kids start school, to extending the hours they stay there,

---

* Daniel B. Wood, "No More Telecommuting? Not a Problem for Most American Workers," *Christian Science Monitor*, March 5, 2013, http://www.csmonitor.com/USA/2013/0305/No-more-telecommuting-Not-a-problem-for-most-American-workers.

to making school year-round, to now proposing state-run boarding schools that take over the role of parents almost completely.

Secretary of Education Arne Duncan argued in support of public boarding schools at the National Summit on Youth Violence Prevention in 2015. Certain kids, he said, the government needs to control "24/7 to really create a safe environment and give them a chance to be successful." *Certain kids.* Not yours. Well, *probably* not yours. Duncan explained that he was talking about kids "where there's not a mom, there's not a dad, there's not a grandma, there's just nobody at home." Actually, that sounds like child abandonment; the state is already allowed to intervene in cases like that. But Duncan didn't talk about the need for more state-run orphanages; he talked about "public boarding schools."

Duncan might have in mind what Buffalo, New York, school board member Carl Paladino has been pushing for: public boarding schools for children, starting in elementary school. "We have teachers and union leaders telling us, 'the problem is with the homes; these kids are in dysfunctional homes.'"* When you consider that the state is pretty dysfunctional itself, particularly in these failing school districts, blaming dysfunctional parents sounds like a classic case of blame-shifting in order to justify a governmental power grab of sweeping proportions. Buffalo, for instance, has the nation's third-highest per-pupil expenditure rate, according to the *Buffalo News.*** The district spent $26,903 per student in 2010, yet its graduation rate of 55 percent in 2014 was nearly twenty points lower than the New York

---

* Carolyn Thompson, "Buffalo Considers Public Boarding Schools to Solve Education Issues," Huffington Post, April 27, 2015, http://www.huffingtonpost.com/2015/04/27/buffalo-public-boarding-schools_n_7152716.html.
** Mary Pasciak, "Buffalo's School Spending Is Nation's Third Highest," *Buffalo News*, September 13, 2012, http://www.buffalonews.com/apps/pbcs.dll/article?aid=/20120913/cityandregion/120919509.

state average. Test scores are well below the state average in virtually all subjects and for all grade levels. When Governor Andrew Cuomo released a list of 177 "failing schools" in the state in his 2015 report "The State of New York's Failing Schools," forty-five out of the fifty-seven schools in the Buffalo public school system were named. That sounds pretty dysfunctional to me. I'd start looking at ways to get students *out* of these schools, not ways to keep them there 24/7.

Whether you work from home, work outside the home, or make parenting your full-time job, we all have this in common: our kids are at home. Oh sure, there may be the occasional sleepover, summer camp, or even boarding school or exchange program for our kids once they're older. We're not, however, packing our kids up and shipping them off a few blocks away at the age of six or seven. Maybe we should forget about the Mommy Wars and find our common ground in defense of parenting itself against outsourcing it to a failing public school system.

19

Having Another Child (or Two)

After your first child has reached the point of sleeping through the night, but before he or she is actually potty-trained, you and your spouse may decide you want to do this all over again. Not that you need our permission, but good for you. In fact, great for you, because not only are fewer people in their twenties having kids, it's even rarer to see them have a second or third child.

I kind of cheated in that I married into a family. It may have taken a few years to become a biological father, but I became "Dad" to my first two kids as soon as I said, "I do," and I have no regrets. In fact, it's too bad every parent can't start out with a child or two that can sleep through the night, talk to you, actually use a restroom, dress themselves, and behave reasonably well in public. It might also help if the kids were as amusing, bright, and lovable as my kids were.

When our third child was born in 2000, I kind of figured that we were done having kids. We never definitively ruled that our baby-making days were over, but we certainly weren't planning on another one. So when my wife approached me about having another baby in the summer of 2004, I wasn't really gung-ho. I also wasn't entirely opposed. I was a little concerned about my wife's age, and with our daughter getting ready to start her senior year of high school it just seemed a little weird to be talking about having another baby.

Still, I really didn't require much convincing. Yeah, I had my concerns, but I like kids. I liked being a dad. So we once again decided to make a baby, and once again, we were successful on the first try. Really successful, as it turned out.

We were excited to find out if we were having a boy or a girl, and the morning of the sonogram appointment I went with my wife to the doctor's office, along with our four-year-old son (our older kids were in school, and likely would have thought it weird to go to their mom's OB-GYN appointment anyway). The doc came in, gelled up my wife's belly, and soon we were looking at blobby images on the video monitor. Sonograms have come a long way in terms of clarity over the years, but I still had a hard time deciphering what I was seeing. It looked like there were two heads there on the monitor, but that couldn't be right. After all, the doctor wasn't saying anything about two babies.

And then, right on cue, he did.

"Most people would have said something by now," he chuckled, "but since you haven't, let me point out that here is Baby A's head and here is Baby B's head."

I felt like I was going to vomit. My wife went pale. The silence was broken by our four-year-old happily exclaiming, "We're having *two* babies?!" Yes, we were, and as it turns out we were totally blindsided by that fact. Okay, I was blindsided. My wife swears she knew something was different about this particular pregnancy, and there was a moment early on where she said she thought she shouldn't be as big as she was that early on, but when a visit to the doctor turned up one heartbeat, I put the thought of twins completely out of my mind.*

It's not that I wasn't excited on some level. I was thrilled that both babies appeared to be healthy, and was really pleased to learn that we were having both a boy and a girl. I think I was just in shock for a while. It wasn't the easiest pregnancy for my wife, either. She was on bed rest for the last several months, and as her due date approached we both waited with anticipation and fear of the unknown. Having an infant is tough, but we both knew we could do it. Having two, though, that was a new experience for both of us. We didn't really know what to expect, other than it being a lot harder than having one child.**

Well, the due date came and went, and once again we headed in to the hospital for labor to be induced. This time around things went much better, although once again the pain meds didn't really do much for my wife. She went into labor right away, and less than four hours after we'd arrived at the hospital our son and daughter were born.

That last sentence makes it sound so easy, but then again I wasn't the one expelling almost sixteen pounds of baby out of my body. I was the one standing by my wife's head, holding her hand (actually, letting her squeeze my hand until I could feel my bones scraping together), and cheering her on while she pushed, breathed, cursed a bit, and pushed some more. My son, weighing seven pounds, six ounces, arrived first, with his eight-pound sister following five minutes later. My wife and I once again went through those tense moments as we waited for the nurses to announce that our kids were healthy and breathing, which thankfully was true for both of them. I picked up our son, gazed at this tiny little person swaddled in a blanket with eyes squinted shut against the bright

---

* Turns out if you're only listening for one heartbeat that may be all that you hear.

** For some reason, a lot of parents of twins call children who aren't twins "singletons." I find this weird, though it would be a great name for a Weezer album.

light, and carried him over to my wife with an ear-to-ear grin on my face. A nurse handed me my daughter and I wrapped her in my arms, holding her up so that my wife could see her. We played "pass the baby" back and forth, each of us taking turns holding one, then the other, then both. My wife and I were laughing and crying, our eyes red and our cheeks sore from our smiles.

While I remember with exquisite clarity that morning in the hospital room when I first laid eyes on my youngest son and daughter, I honestly don't remember much about the following six months. The twins went through a period where they had trouble sleeping, as all babies do, but none of our old tricks—rocking, singing, walking around with them in our arms—worked. We had to be more creative: like putting them in their car seats and placing them on top of a running clothes dryer. The vibrations would lull them to sleep most of the time, but it also meant there were many nights when I'd sit in our laundry room in a small chair in front of the dryer, a hand on each car seat, fitfully dozing while my family slept upstairs.

The lack of sleep was, for me anyway, always the hardest part of having an infant. The benefits, however, more than make up for the low-grade exhaustion you might experience during the first few months. I was captivated by these two remarkable creatures, conceived together (or at least over the same weekend) and occupying the same space for nine months, but so different in so many different ways. At the time, I was working evenings, so I could spend my mornings and early afternoons with the babies, and I was fascinated by their emerging personalities. My daughter was a ham who loved to make people laugh, while my son was much more serious and would soak in the world through his dark blue eyes. One morning when the three of us were curled up on the couch together, an infant in each arm, it struck me that my kids were literally keeping my hands full. I didn't mind a bit, though I was overjoyed when they started sleeping through the night.

With five kids now in the house, there was little free time to speak of. Priorities changed. I went an entire football season without knowing what the records were for my favorite teams, and most of my knowledge of current pop culture was replaced in my head with every line of dialogue from *Little Einsteins*. I couldn't name a single song on the Billboard Top 10, but I could tell you the track listing for The Wiggles' *Hoop De Do! It's a Wiggly Party* without even looking at the CD case.

I realize that having five kids is something of an anomaly these days. The size of the U.S. family has been steadily shrinking for decades, and in 2010 the U.S. Census recorded an average of 2.58 people (not kids, but people) per household. At one point we had a household of seven, or nearly triple the size of the average American family, but since our oldest daughter and son have left the house we're now down to a household of five. There are sacrifices that come with having a larger family. Every one of my kids knows what it's like to share a room with a sibling, for instance. Taking five kids on vacation really narrows your options, because of logistics and cost. I'd love to be able to take family trips to far-off destinations, but seven plane tickets, hotels, meals, etc., add up quickly. When, after almost ten years of marriage, we took our first family vacation, we drove to North Carolina and rented a house near (not on) the beach for a week, eating most of our meals at "home" and staying away from the money-sucking activities like mini-golf and outlet malls. Heck, even going to the movies is a rare occasion in our family. It's much cheaper to wait for the DVD to come out and buy some popcorn at the store.

Dance Fever

The sacrifices are nothing, however, in comparison with the rewards. The greatest thing about being a parent is helping your child grow up and become an independent individual. We encouraged our kids' interests, even if we didn't share them. I will admit that when my oldest daughter wanted to play the drums, I was less than enthused. But my father-in-law bought her a drum kit, and while I might have been willing to put my foot down about buying a set of drums, I wasn't about to cross my wife, my daughter, and my father-in-law (who's a pretty big guy and whose nickname is The Torch).*

Our kids' curiosity led them to exploring guitar, painting, soccer, football, basketball, baseball, karate, Cub Scouts, swimming, and dance. When my youngest son was four, he asked if he could take ballet lessons. My wife and I had been thinking about getting him into gymnastics, but he was adamant. It was ballet he wanted, not tumbling.

I'm old enough to remember NFL running back Herschel Walker dancing with the Fort Worth Ballet. I saw dancer Mikhail Baryshnikov take on the KGB (with the help of Gregory Hines) in *White Nights*. I had no problem with my son wanting to take ballet. I just wasn't sure why he'd become so interested in ballet. He couldn't tell me why, he just *was*.

So, I signed him up for a class. We went on a Saturday morning, and throughout the hour he dutifully followed the instructor's directions, but with a deep, dark scowl on his face. After the class was dismissed, he came stomping over to me and looked me in the face.

"This is *not* what I expected, Dad."

"What did you expect?"

"Dancing!"

I explained that you had to train your body and learn the moves before you could dance, but he looked disgusted with the whole thing.

On our way home he stared out the window; suddenly his eyes brightened. "I know what I want to take," he announced. "It's not ballet."

"No? What is it then?"

"Free form jazz dance!"

"Well, little dude, I don't know that the Parks and Recreation Department offers a free form jazz dance class." He looked heartbroken.

"But here's the thing," I added. "It's free form, right? So, you don't really need a class. You just need music."

---

* This is true, though he got the nickname because of his welding abilities, not because he ever set any sons-in-law on fire.

"Jazz music," he interjected.

"Right, of course. Can't have a free form jazz dance party without some jazz music. And as it happens, I've got some jazz music at home."

And that is how the tradition of the Daddy Dance Party began in our house. After we got home, I explained to my wife that what our son really wanted to do was free form jazz dance instead of a structured ballet class. Then we fired up Miles Davis's "Spanish Key" and my son and I started expressively dancing our way around our living room. Soon my wife joined in, along with our youngest daughter. Eventually even our older kids decided they weren't too cool to dance, and for an hour or so we all goofily grooved to the music. Our kids quickly decided that Miles Davis wasn't really their thing, but they did like Parliament Funkadelic and Deee-Lite.

I might not remember what I need to pick up at the grocery store or where I left my sunglasses, but that's unimportant compared to memories of bopping along to "Groove Is in the Heart" while my four-year-old son attempts to do the Robot and his siblings cheer him on. My life is exponentially richer and more complete thanks to each and every one of my children, including the sweet moves I picked up from a little guy who just wanted to dance.

What Would Ward Cleaver Do?

He did it. Without a second child for Ward and June, there would have been no Theodore "Beaver" Cleaver, an incalculable loss for us all.

20

School Days

ere's the good news about when your children get old enough to go to school: you don't have to go with them.

Until back-to-school night, and then anything that you didn't like about your childhood school experience will come rushing back to you. You might even be asked to sit on those kid-sized chairs.

Schools seem to require a lot more from parents now than they did when we attended—and I don't just mean tuition for those who choose to send their kids to private school. Maybe there was never a golden era where parents could send their kids to the neighborhood public school and rest easy knowing they would get a fine education that would prepare them for college and the workplace. But it certainly feels like relying on the neighborhood school is a much bigger crapshoot than it used to be. Over the past four decades, Gallup respondents have become increasingly likely to say that today's students receive a "worse education" than they themselves did.* In 1975, more than 60 percent of respondents said they had a "great deal" or "quite a lot" of confidence in public schools. By 2014, only 26 percent of respondents said the same.

Whether your child goes to a public or a private school, you'll probably find that the teachers expect you to be a lot more engaged with what's going on than your parents were. This is likely terrific for your child, but it's a lot more pressure on you.

 My younger son's preschool teacher is perhaps the nicest, sweetest soul imaginable. And yet, quite a few mornings this year, we have had the same uncomfortable exchange:

"Good morning! Did he bring it?"

I stare blankly and wonder what memo in the backpack I have failed to examine. Remember that feeling in grade school when you didn't bring your homework? All of a sudden, at age thirty-something, you're right back with your deer-in-the-headlights expression, square in the sights of a disapproving teacher.

"Did he bring the..."

She's gently repeating the question, but she already knows I haven't brought it. We've done this dance before. Mr. Geraghty never reads the memos.

It's not just once-a-week show-and-tell, although we've forgotten that one plenty of times, too. No, now preschool and school revolve around class projects, which all involve bringing in something from home.

"Did he bring the coat hanger?"

"Um," I say, wondering if there's some way I can somehow magically *will* the coat hanger into existence. Or I can claim I left it in the car, run back to my car, drive home, and pick up the forgotten object.

---

* Catherine Rampell, "Actually, Public Education Is Getting Better, Not Worse," *Washington Post*, September 18, 2014.

Did I get that memo? Did my wife mention the memo? Was there a memo? Was there an e-mail? Did some carrier pigeon get shot out of the sky?

"Coat hanger?"

"Yes, it is for the class project that we talked about in the memo," she will explain patiently, with only a few stray molecules of disappointment in her voice, "because all the kids are bringing a part to class to build a scale model of a nuclear reactor, and we plan on building one like MacGyver."

Ugh. So now the class project that was supposed to end with a controlled mushroom cloud—or a baking-soda-and-vinegar volcano eruption, or transforming lead into gold through alchemy, or something else spectacularly educational and mind-expanding—is on hold because I didn't know I was supposed to bring in a coat hanger.

I got the kids out the door on time; packed a lunch; got them into the necessary jackets, hats, gloves; brought the necessary pocket change for the weekly give-to-charity exercise; brought the freshly laundered sleeping mat for nap time; got them into the car; made sure their seatbelts were on; fought traffic; battled the idiots who check their cell phones while sitting at a red light in the left-turn-only lane, but don't bother to look up at the light, and use up half the window of the green light before they get moving—and all of that is moot, because it's 8 a.m. and I'm already a bad father because I forgot the coat hanger.

The other parents who arrive simultaneously and I communicate entirely through facial expressions. There's the *I-remembered-my-child's-coat-hanger* look, which I notice tends to come from moms. The other dads give me a variation of the "can you believe we pay tuition for this endless list of assignments?" look.

School now involves a lot more "projects" than I remember. My friends' child had a class project that was meant to teach them about foreign cultures; they had to bring to school ten objects from the same foreign country. Ten? What, are they opening up a Pier One store in the school cafeteria? Running an import-export business? As they lamented their sudden search for Japanese objects, I asked, "Is it too late to change to China or Taiwan? Because *everything's* made there."

Assured that the choice of Japan was incontestable, I offered, "How about ten Pokémon cards? What about going to the sushi place and getting ten sets of chopsticks?" (As you can imagine, my friends find me enormously helpful.)

It's fascinating to hear the teachers' "don't do your child's homework for them" warning coupled with project assignments that are pretty unimaginable for grade schoolers to complete on their own. (*"To complete your project display, borrow your dad's hot glue gun and some turpentine...if you run out of turpentine, steal the car keys and drive to the nearest Walmart."*) Still, if project-mania is a teacher's passive-aggressive way of attempting to mandate parental involvement in a child's schoolwork, I can't begrudge a teacher that much.

There's a broad cultural consensus that teachers have an extremely tough job, but for the wrong reasons. A teacher gets access to a child—well, dozens of them—for about six, maybe seven hours a day. They don't get to control what happens to that child after they leave the school grounds. Maybe the parents are really invested in their child's education, maybe they aren't. Maybe the neighborhood between school and home is safe, maybe it isn't. Maybe the kids came to school well-rested, fully fed, and given a steady cultural diet of books and educational videos and field trips; maybe the home life is an unstable, chaotic mess. Teachers rightfully ask just how much they can educate a child with insufficient support on the home front.

My older son's first grade teacher had the good idea of stopping by the homes of every child in the first month of school; she wanted to get a sense of the home life for every child—do they have siblings? How do they behave at home? Do they have a lot of books in the house? Okay, it's possible that she just wanted to get home decorating ideas, or she was extremely nosy. But I liked the concept. Parents see their kids as spectacular geniuses and creative prodigies, just waiting to be unlocked. I think every parent desperately hopes for a teacher who will see that same unrealized potential, and devote a portion of the school year to unleashing it.

The home visit from my son's teacher couldn't have gone any better. I am not making this up when I say my older son, entirely unbidden, went and got out the chess set and started teaching his little brother how to play chess. We could not have created a more idyllic image of our home life if we had rehearsed it. Best of all, as the teacher described her active role in the local chapter of a national teachers' union, she didn't notice the picture of me with Dick Cheney, my pile of *National Review* magazines, and all of my other professional knickknacks that might as well say "THIS MAN DESPISES ALL TEACHERS' UNIONS AND EVERYTHING THEY STAND FOR; GRADE HIS SON ACCORDINGLY."

My son has had good teachers and not-so-good ones. If a good teacher can be a miracle worker, a bad teacher can be a weapon of mass mind destruction.

How the hell do you make human history—with its heroes, madmen, wars, betrayals, world-changing inventions, dramatic twists of fate, and epic story leading up to today—boring? How do you make the world of science—with praying mantises eating their mates, mysterious black holes deep in space, long-lost monsters of the deep sea, and chemicals that can explode—dreadful drudgery? How do you make literature—the realm of Ray Bradbury, Jonathan Swift, Mark Twain, and H. G. Wells— a joyless chore?

Look at the nonfiction bestseller list: it's history, science, autobiography, philosophy, politics. There's a special place in hell for any teacher who can make a kid hate reading.

The late genius Andrew Breitbart declared of the perpetually sputtering Republican Party, "If you can't sell freedom and liberty, you suck." If you, as a teacher, can't sell any aspect of the entire far-reaching and fascinating realm of human knowledge—your subject matter! The professional role you chose!—to a young mind...well, you stink, too.

Bad Boys...or Bad Teachers (or Bureaucrats)

As my sons grow older, I'm particularly on alert for schools and teachers that simply don't know how to handle boys. I'm too much of a layman to offer a definitive take on whether American parents are over-medicating our kids, and whether a lot of diagnoses of attention deficit-disorder are merely high-energy boys being shoehorned into the conformity of a society that doesn't know how to accept them as they are. I do know that, by and large, boys like to run around, play in mud, climb things, occasionally hit each other, pick up bugs, stick things up their nose, and do other things that a lot of professional middle-aged women educators find rambunctious and uncouth.

I know not every public school teacher has turned into a hypersensitive panic-inclined ninny, but sometimes it seems that way. In 2013, a second grader in Baltimore's Park Elementary School was suspended for two days after he chewed his breakfast pastry into the shape of a gun. In 2014 in Columbus, Ohio, a ten-year-old boy was suspended for three days for pretending his finger was a gun. Same thing for a first grader in Colorado the following year. In 2011, a thirteen-year-old was allegedly handcuffed and hauled to juvenile detention for burping in class.*

In 2010, the principal of the junior high school in Forest Hills, New York, called the police after a twelve-year-old girl doodled on her desk in class. No threatening message, just "I love my friends Abby and Faith. Lex was here 2/1/10 :)" in green marker.

Get a farshtunken** grip, educators. You're supposed to be the grown-ups here. In fact, if public school teachers and principals feel like they're not treated with sufficient respect by the rest of society, it's probably oft-shared tales like this one that drive the derision. What some idiotic principal deems a commonsense, consistent application of a "zero tolerance" policy looks to us like either politically correct hysteria or a pint-sized dictator mad with his power over our children.

---

* "Student Arrested for Burping, Lawsuit Claims," CBS News, December 1, 2011, http://www.cbsnews.com/news/student-arrested-for-burping-lawsuit-claims/.
** Yiddish for "stinking"—a useful substitute for the other F-word.

Boys like playing all kinds of games with "guns"—Star Wars, Transformers, G.I. Joe, Ghostbusters, cowboys, pirates, spacemen and aliens, hunters…why have we decided to literally criminalize this once-common aspect of boyhood? Do we really think that by clamping down on finger guns and sandwich pistols, we'll prevent the next school shooting? Will we next ban Matchbox cars to prevent car accidents?

If a seven-year-old with a peanut butter sandwich gun frightens you, then you really don't want to see my reaction to the news that you've decided to turn my child into a national headline over your ammophobia. Even if we parents acquiesce to this philosophy that anything resembling a firearm—even appendages—must be treated like Voldemort, the common object that must not be named, you as a teacher or principal have a whole arsenal of disciplinary options in front of you! (I know, I know, that martial metaphor just frightened you because it's a trigger word—whoops, did it again!) What's with the knee-jerk suspensions? Is there some trapdoor built into the floor of your office? You're a middle school principal, not NFL Commissioner Roger Goodell. That office chair under your tush ain't the Iron Throne.

Even aside from the disciplinary policies, parents of boys run into nagging doubts that some corners of the school system treat them as some sort of alien creature. I remember reading a perhaps apocryphal tale of a father attending a back-to-school night and hearing a high school English teacher lament that all of the girls in the class were doing well, while all of the boys were performing poorly and barely paying attention in class; she lamented that they all might have attention deficit disorder. The father asked to see the curriculum for the year and was given a list of works by Jane Austen, Louisa May Alcott, Edith Wharton, Charlotte Brontë, Virginia Woolf.…

Gee, why would teenage boys seem bored and uninterested with a selection of works about social propriety and etiquette in England a century ago?

Why do some teachers of literature seem determined to avoid any works that young men might actually want to read? Sherlock Holmes? Huck Finn? *Treasure Island*? *Brave New World*? *Lord of the Flies*? Edgar

Allan Poe's morbid twists? If you've instituted some sort of "only dead women authors" rule, Mary Shelley wrote *Frankenstein*! Most of Ayn Rand's novels are longer than a Peter Jackson film adaptation of Robert A. Caro's Lyndon Johnson biographical volumes,* but at least her Objectivist philosophies would spur a passionate debate in class.

I'm sure most teachers do their best. We've given them one of our society's biggest responsibilities, and they're forced to work in a system that is bizarrely antiquated and vociferously defensive of the status quo. Sometimes it seems like the only innovation we see in some school systems is their new, groundbreaking ways of resisting innovation.

The modern form of education doesn't make a lot of sense. Instead of encountering grown-ups and witnessing all the various ways that they work and contribute to society, most kids encounter only a handful of adults each day: their parents, maybe the school bus driver, their teacher, and maybe their soccer coach, dance instructor, or karate sensei. We wall kids off from the rest of society, so they marinate in the no-holds-barred social circle of their peers—particularly in junior high and high school. We all know kids can be gasp-inducingly cruel to each other, and those malicious pack instincts only intensify during the hormonal hurricane of puberty.

You've probably witnessed the recent pop-cultural spate of dystopian science fiction showcasing teenagers largely living on their own—the Divergent series, Maze Runner, etc.... What makes these stories dystopian isn't the post-apocalyptic setting, crumbling buildings, Orwellian rules, or hellish landscapes. No, it's that the teenagers are in charge of themselves, with that thin tendril of adult supervision removed, and every teen impulse fully unbridled from bullies, teenage crushes, social hierarchy and ostracizing of outsiders, tsunami-force

---

* I'm kidding, of course. Scientists have determined that for director Peter Jackson—who created an eight-hour film trilogy out of a three-hundred-page work, *The Hobbit*—to make a film out of Robert Caro's three-thousand-page, five-volume biographical series, production work would have needed to start before the Big Bang.

sex drives, and inexplicable waves of confusion and anger. Teens devour these books in part because they relate to those struggling but determined protagonists.

It's amazing that anyone comes out of the teenage years with a good head on his shoulders.

You might be lucky and your child will get good teachers almost every year. You're almost certain to get at least one stinker in there. You certainly remember yours. It can be a pain, but it always passes. And the biggest educator in your child's life is you.

What Would Ward Cleaver Do?

Ward lived before the collapse of public education, so he could send his kids off to school pretty confident that they would learn something and that he wouldn't have to turn up at class every day with whatever assignment the teachers had given the parents. Glory days.

PART V
Dads Out and Proud

Be a Dad. Don't be "Mom's Assistant." . . .
Spend time with your kids.
It won't take away your manhood, it will give it to you.

—Louis C.K.

21

Raising a
Responsible Rebel

In South Carolina, a working single mom is arrested because her nine-year-old daughter was playing unsupervised in a nearby park. A couple in Florida faced felony charges because their eleven-year-old had to wait outside the house for ninety minutes one afternoon after school (the kid had food, access to water, and shelter for that traumatic hour and a half). A mom and dad in the D.C. suburb of Silver Spring, Maryland, faced multiple investigations from Child Protective Services and the police for allowing their children to walk to nearby parks and explore their neighborhood without adult supervision. A mom in Chicago was found guilty of child neglect after allowing her three children to play in a park adjacent to their apartment while she checked on them through the window every few minutes. These are just a few of the modern-day horror stories found at Lenore Skenazy's website Free Range Kids, and she's never running low on new material, unfortunately. We've made it downright dangerous to let your kid have any degree of independence.

It didn't used to be this way. Back in the 1970s, psychologist Roger Hart delved into the lives of kids in a small Vermont town. Over the course of two years Hart interviewed virtually every child between the ages of four and twelve, and turned his research into his dissertation, which in turn inspired quite a bit of attention in the scientific press, as well as a BBC documentary on children and play. Three decades later, Hart returned to the rural town to talk to the original subjects and, when possible, their own kids as well.

What he found is deeply depressing. Back in the seventies, kids in the town roamed for blocks. They ventured off the sidewalk and played in the woods or down by the river, and always without parental supervision. In fact, parents often had no real idea where their kids were at any given time. The older kids were supposed to look out for the younger ones (with an almost unwritten rule that some bossiness was to be expected). All of that had changed when he returned in the mid-2000s, even though the town itself still had the same low crime rate and relatively tight-knit community. Now there was little free time for kids, and it certainly wasn't unsupervised. Play dates were scheduled, instead of kids just hanging out after school. What it meant to be a kid had changed, and not for the better. The parents that Hart had studied thirty years ago looked back nostalgically on their youth, but that didn't change the fact that they were raising their kids much differently.

Hart spoke to the *Atlantic*'s Hanna Rosin for her feature "The Over-Protected Kid," and wasn't quite sure why the change had been so quick and so prevalent. "There's a fear," Hart said, "an exaggeration of the dangers, a loss of trust that isn't totally explainable."

I actually think the explanation can be found in the growth of the twenty-four-hour news cycle and our brains' inability to process the never-ending litany of horrors shown to us on our cable news channels, tablets, and smartphones. Things have gotten exponentially worse with the rise of social media. I see this all the time in the gun control debate. Anti-gun advocates are constantly talking about the "epidemic" rates of gun-related violence in the United States, and how "something" (which really means something anti-gun) needs to be done. These advocates and the reporters who cover them seldom mention the fact that gun-related violent crime has declined dramatically over the past two decades (and of course, when homicides spiked in cities like Baltimore, New York, and Hartford in 2015, those same anti-gun critics failed to mention that the increases happened *after* sweeping gun control laws were passed in Maryland, New York, and Connecticut in 2013). We are, in fact, doing "something" about violent crime, because we're seeing a lot less of it. Yet, according to a 2013 Pew Research Center poll, only 12 percent of those surveyed said that crime had gone down over the past two decades. By comparison, the 2014 Chapman University Survey on American Fears found that more than 20 percent of survey respondents believe Bigfoot is real. That's right, more Americans believe there's a population of ape-like creatures wandering around the forests of Oregon than know that the country they live in has become much less violent over their lifetime.

The Survey on American Fears also found that people who watch TV news and true crime shows tend to be more afraid, which makes sense. If the vast majority of what you watch is crime-related, it's probably natural to think that we live in a hellish landscape of mayhem and horror, even if it's not evident in your daily life (aside from what you see on television). Which is not to say that threats don't exist. Crime, even if crime rates are down, is a fact of life. But the fact that we live in a world where criminal behavior exists is no reason to deny kids a proper childhood by always insisting they remain under constant adult supervision. I want my kids to have a childhood close to mine; with independence, freedom, curiosity, and responsibility. My goal as a parent isn't to make sure that every day is "the best day ever" for my kids. It's to make sure that when they're adults, they're ready to take on the real world.

Sometimes it feels like I'm raising my kids to be rebels against the prevailing culture. Responsible rebels, but rebels nonetheless. The "Free Range Kids" movement, popularized by Lenore Skenazy, is full of parents and kids who are going against the grain, so it's not as if I'm the only one. And frankly, for a lot of parents, raising a "free range" kid is more of a necessity than a choice.

When my wife was a single mom, she had to raise self-reliant, responsible kids. At the age of nine my oldest daughter could run to the corner store in Camden, New Jersey, and buy basic groceries, like a loaf of bread or a dozen eggs. That's the way it is for many families. Helicopter parenting is a luxury they can't afford, but that doesn't mean their kids are worse off than a child who was shuttled and smothered with constant supervision and a never-ending stream of piano lessons, karate classes, and scheduled play dates.

I've never believed my kids should have a more sheltered childhood than I had. Luckily, when I moved my family to northern Virginia, our neighborhood had a number of military families whose kids were trained in responsible childhood freedom. It wasn't unusual for packs of kids to roam the woods at night with flashlights playing a game called "Manhunt," or for my then-ten-year-old son and his friends to walk a mile and a half to 7-Eleven in the afternoons.

Even in that bucolic setting, though, my wife would still get random calls from the neighbors when they saw our youngest daughter riding her bike alone on the sidewalk less than a hundred feet from our house. At least they called my wife and not Child Protective Services, for which I am eternally grateful.

I grew up in the suburbs, mostly south of Oklahoma City, along with a two-year spell in a small town in New Jersey about twenty miles west of New York City. My childhood sounds very much like the one Roger Hart witnessed. At seven, I was riding my bike to my elementary school to take advantage of the playground on the weekend. A year later I was walking alone several blocks to the Friendly's restaurant in the small downtown of Ridgewood, New Jersey,* for a lunch of clam chowder and

---

* I've got a lot of great memories of my time in Ridgewood, but there's one thing that still gets to me. I could walk to the movie theater, take myself to lunch, visit the library by myself, and so on, but I wasn't allowed to play arcade games. The town has an ordinance (still on the books last time I checked) that requires video games for profit to be licensed by the town, and "No license shall permit any of the devices regulated under this article to be used by any person under the

a grilled cheese sandwich. Every now and then my mom and dad would join me on one of my adventures, but for the most part I was on my own. I knew my phone number, I knew my address, and I knew where I was going and how to get back home, whether it was a trip to the library, the town's swimming pool, or my friend Pete's house. I was a latchkey kid, and I had a great time growing up.

My parents did a great job of preparing me for the real world, because they allowed me to explore it as a kid. Sure, there were some issues. Older kids in the neighborhood tended to give us younger ones a hard time, at least until they got to the age where they discovered girls. Generally speaking, though, boredom was our biggest issue, and that was always only a temporary problem. Even with all of that freedom I never felt neglected. We were an affectionate family, and as the youngest I received more than my share. I knew my parents loved me, and my mom and I were really close, especially after my parents divorced. I never went through a period where I rebelled against my mom's authority, though as I got older I did have my periods of typical teenage idiocy.

Beyond giving me the liberty to explore the world I lived in, my parents also encouraged me in my love of reading. That allowed me to explore the world beyond my neighborhood, and the more I read, the more curious about the world I became, which made me want to read and learn even more. I became fascinated with American history through the Childhood of Famous Americans series.* For a while after reading Roger Kahn's *The Boys of Summer* I was as big a fan of the 1950s

---

age of sixteen years." For two years the only opportunities I had to play arcade games were the evenings we'd drive to neighboring Hoboken to eat at a diner. This particular diner had a Pac-Man game in the lobby, but the game, for some reason, was in German. I still remember my first trip to the arcade in Crossroads Mall after we moved back to Oklahoma. I was awestruck as I soaked in the rows of displays, joysticks, and buttons...all finally available for me to play. I might have even wept a little as I put a quarter into a *Spy Hunter* game, overjoyed at doing something other than eating dots and running from ghosts.

* Crispus Attucks was a particular favorite of mine, and I remember developing this weird prepubescent crush on Clara Barton after reading her biography. I wouldn't feel the same way about a woman until I saw Lea Thompson in *Howard the Duck*.

Brooklyn Dodgers as I was the 1986 Boston Red Sox.* I learned more about science from the adventures of Danny Dunn, Boy Scientist than I did from Bill Nye, Science Guy. I always had a paperback with me, and would even read at concerts in between the opening act and the main event. I distinctly remember killing time waiting for Bon Jovi by thumbing through a copy of S. E. Hinton's *The Outsiders*.

I don't know that any of my kids caught the reading bug quite as bad as I did, but every one of my children reads for pleasure, just as my wife and I do. My youngest daughter shocked me by reading *The Lord of the Rings* trilogy when she was eleven. My youngest son loved books on Egyptian and Greek mythology, and I read aloud the tales of Perseus, Heracles, and Theseus. After a few Minotaur-related nightmares, we switched to *Aesop's Fables*, which, I explained, were kind of like myths, only with fewer monsters and vengeful gods. I'm not a perfect parent, and I don't have perfect kids. I'm okay with that. I'm not aiming for perfection. I want my kids to grow up to be happy, healthy, responsible, and productive adults. I want them to think *for* themselves, not just *about* themselves. They don't have to vote like me, though we do talk politics. They don't have to own a gun, though I've taught all my children how to shoot safely and responsibly. They don't even have to eat meat, even though we're raising our own hogs, goats, and sheep now. It's my job as a parent to equip my kids with the tools they need to live a purposeful life of their own, not to turn them into little mini-me's.

I want my children to be able to stand up to what Charlton Heston called the "pervasive social subjugation" of our modern-day thought police. To do that, he told a crowd at Harvard Law School in 1999, one had to learn to disobey. "Peaceably, yes," Moses told his flock, "Respectfully, of course. Nonviolently, absolutely. But when told how to think or

---

* This ultimately led to my trading a 1986 Fleer Michael Jordan card for a 1956 Topps Jackie Robinson card. The Jordan card is now worth a couple thousand bucks, depending on condition, while a Jackie Robinson card in similar condition to mine can be found for a couple hundred bucks. But I still have that card, and it still means more to me than the Jordan card ever could. Looking back, I'm proud that a twelve-year-old me understood the difference between a great player and a history maker.

what to say or how to behave, we don't. We disobey the social protocol that stifles and stigmatizes personal freedom."

I don't expect my kids to turn out just like me or their mom, but if they turn out a little like Charlton Heston I'd be thrilled.

What Would Ward Cleaver Do?

Self-reliance, independence—these were some of the things we used to take for granted in the American character. Ward had it—and he would have wanted it in his sons.

22

Dads Get It Done

 You would not have expected a commercial for Peanut Butter Cheerios to be a groundbreaking statement about modern fatherhood.

It started out as a Canadian ad for Peanut Butter Cheerios, and was changed to a Honey Nut Cheerios ad for U.S. audiences. The U.S. version ran on *Sunday Night Football* on NBC. It is two minutes in length—way longer than the usual thirty-second ad—and contains more dialogue and action than some half-hour sitcoms. It is better seen than transcribed, but for those who missed it, this was the dialogue:

[A sleeping man awakens to a child with a horse's head mask jumping on his chest.]
Dad: HUH!
Son: You awake?

Dad: Yeah, of course I'm awake. Is that a new mask?

Son: Oh yeah.

Dad: I love it. It's really creepy.

Son: I know, right?

Dad: Yeah, good stuff.

Son: Thanks.

[The dad tosses his son off his stomach.]

Dad [to camera]: Hey. Let me introduce myself. My name is—

Daughter: DAD!

Dad: And proud of it. And all dads should be.

[The dad gets out of bed and begins walking through the house, offering a monologue to the camera while getting his kids ready for the day.]

Daughter: Dad! Dad! Dad! Dad! Dad!

Dad: Why? You know why. Kids think we're awesome. We get our hands messy. We tell hilarious jokes.

[to sleeping son]

Hey, Nolan. We got to get up, buddy.

[to camera]

We never say no to dress up. We build the best forts. We do work-work and we do homework. We lead by example and we blow their minds.

Son: I can't believe he's his father!

Dad: [to son] I know! That is called a "plot twist"!

[to camera]

Being awesome isn't about breaking rules. It's about making them. Hot stuff coming through!

[He hands his wife a coffee.]

Dad: [to camera] Wife *and* the coffee.

And breakfast is for breakfast.

[to teenage son]

Hey, Nolan, give me a look here.

[He adjusts his son's cap.]

Dad: Suggestion, that's a boy, that's a man.

[back to camera]

But it's also for lunch, dinner, and midnight snacks.

Scraped knees aren't boo-boos, they are badges of bravery on the playground.

[to teenage daughter]

Hey, Victoria? That profile pic? Awesome.

[He heads outside.]

Dad: When you're a dad, hugs can be bear hugs, but they can also be high-fives, fist-bumps and next-level handshakes.

[lifts son from backyard swingset]

Kids. They're our best friends. They're our greatest fans.

[pats son]

Buddy, you've been gaining muscle mass, nice!

[back to camera]

And they look to us the same way we look at superheroes. Up. Because we're taller. Now, dad-hood isn't always easy. When a rule is broken, we're the enforcement.

[to son]

Hey, buddy, it's garbage day.

[back to camera]

But when a heart is broken, we're the reinforcement. And we wouldn't have it any other way. Because being a dad is awesome. Just like new Peanut Butter Cheerios is awesome. That's why it's the official cereal of dad-hood.

[He pauses in the driveway of his house.]

Dad: And this? This, my friends…[long pause] This is how to dad.

[He raises two fingers in either the peace sign or Churchill's victory sign, and we see a montage of him dancing with his family, holding the Cheerios box.]

The ad received a roaring, enthusiastic response on Facebook. As of this writing, the ad has 1.6 million views on Facebook. The National Fatherhood Initiative raved, "The new commercial on YouTube reveals exactly what we at NFI hope other brands will do…show a dad as a fully functioning and capable parent…without degrading anyone in the family." The Parents Television Council saluted it: "This commercial bucks the unfortunate media trend of depicting dads and bumbling, clueless, incompetent, lazy men." AdAge stated that "it's about time" commercials moved beyond buffoonish portrayals of fathers.

Fascinatingly, the marketing firm that made the ad said they hadn't aimed to tap into the sentiment at all:

> Josh Stein, executive creative director for Tribal's Toronto office, says that while portraying an empowered dad was always at the back of his mind, he didn't set out to buck the traditional "bumbling dad" stereotype, which has been the fodder for much of the social media discussion surrounding the ad. "I'd be lying if I said that the goal of this work was to generate an international conversation around the portrayal of dads, but our work seems to have aligned with that parallel conversation," he says. "Our goal was just to do the best campaign to launch this new product in the slowing cereal category, with dad as our primary target."*

Naturally, Salon.com hated it, continuing their Cal-Ripken-esque record-breaking uninterrupted streak of consecutive wrong takes. (I'm really looking forward to Salon's review of this book.)

"When you define dad as the cool one, as the one who can get his hands 'messy,' you are firmly pigeonholing mom in her role as the lame one," lamented Salon contributor Hayley Krischer.**

Oh, FFS, as they say on the Internet.***

Pardon my reference to the F-bomb, but it's a good segue to a fascinating documentary released in 2010, entitled *The Other F Word*, showcasing

---

* Molly Soat, "Cheerios Leverages the Power of 'Dadvertising,'" Marketing News Weekly, January 13, 2015, https://www.ama.org/publications/eNewsletters/Marketing-News-Weekly/Pages/cheerios-how-to-dad.aspx.
** Hayley Krischer, "I Hate When My Husband Tries to Be a 'Cool Dad': Why You Shouldn't Believe the New Cheerios Commercial," Salon, July 28, 2014, http://www.salon.com/2014/07/28/dont_believe_that_new_cheerios_commercial_why_i_hate_the_myth_of_the_cool_dad/.
*** For you-know-what's sake.

the lives of punk-rock stars of years past in their current lives as fathers. Produced by Cristan Reilly and directed by Andrea Nevins, the film reveals what some dads may have long suspected: sooner or later, every man ends up in a minivan singing, "The wheels on the bus go round and round" to his child—even Art Alexakis of Everclear.

To many audiences, the punk-rock stars depicted in the film—Black Flag's Ron Reyes, Mark Hoppus of Blink 182, pro skater Tony Hawk— embodied everything cool, revolutionary, anarchic, and hedonistic, a vehement, uncompromising rebellion against all forms of authority...and now they find themselves the authority. The film is funny and sweet, and a bit more serious when the rockers discuss their own painful childhoods and often absent-fathers, and how this motivates them to be such dedicated fathers.

Flea, bassist for the Red Hot Chili Peppers—known for anarchic antics such as performing completely naked at the 1999 Woodstock concert—declares, "The classic parent attitude to a kid is like, 'I brought you into this world. I gave you life!' It's like, I just think completely opposite. My kids gave me life, you know. They gave me a reason."

Jim Lindberg, frontman of the punk-rock band Pennywise who wrote a book in 2007 entitled *Punk Rock Dad* that largely inspired the film, says at one point, "When we were younger, we were all nihilistic, and didn't care. Live for today. Live fast. I thought we were going to change the world." Lindberg concludes at the end of the film: "Maybe the way we change the world is by raising better kids and being more attentive to those kids."

If these men can adapt to the demands of fatherhood, any young man can. These rockers' self-image and sense of identity revolved around opposing everything traditionally associated with being a father—responsibility, stability, commitment, devotion, discipline—perhaps even the concept of lifelong love. Maybe all of those concepts didn't need such an across-the-board rejection. Maybe they just needed a little refinement, an adjustment to make a little room for what remains of that youthful anarchic spirit.

One rocker who didn't show up in *The Other F Word* but would have fit in quite well is Duff McKagan, formerly the bassist of Guns N' Roses, perhaps the most notorious hard-rock band of the late 1980s and early 1990s. The era of Guns N' Roses' musical world domination epitomizes every VH1 *Behind the Music* cliché—infighting, rivalries, runaway egos, rampant drug use and addiction, promiscuity that would make Hugh Hefner blush. McKagan describes drinking ten bottles of wine per day until his pancreas burst and he nearly died in emergency surgery.

That rather intense wake-up call from his body—and perhaps his soul—dramatically altered the trajectory of his life, and in the following years, he completed an amazing transformation: he got sober, went back to school, learned how to manage his money, fell in love, became a father—oh, and formed a new band, Velvet Revolver.

One of the fascinating confessions is that even when he was at the heights of rock and roll success, living a life of debauchery and hedonistic excess that could tempt any man, a part of his heart ached to be a stable, trusted, loving father:

> Even during my times of trial and extreme drug and alcohol abuse, I held out hope that one day I'd be that guy who was the head of a family—the steady guider, the calm and strong voice. As a consequence, I am a hopeless romantic when it comes to my wife and two daughters. The imagery that has been forever ingrained in my head by *It's a Wonderful Life* will never leave. My girls think I am totally corny, but I don't care. I am who I am. I can get bummed out sometimes when things don't work out like they did for George Bailey, but waiting for my family at the airport filled me with joy...*

All that glitters is not gold. Maybe you'll reach the heights of fame and fortune—but will it be worth it without someone to share it with and leave it to? Who do you want to come home to when the cheering crowd gets into their cars and leaves?

---

* Duff McKagan, *How to Be a Man* (Boston: DeCapo Press, 2015), 26.

In 2010, a quartet offered a gangster rap video entitled "Dad Life," with seemingly menacing lyrics about their suburban lives of creased dockers, large lawnmowers, work in the yard garden, minivans, backyard barbecues, and watching Disney videos with their daughters.

"I roll hard in the yard with my 60-inch cut, zero turn radius, my neighbors say what?"*

Whatever you think of political correctness, the creative class of our culture increasingly takes steps to avoid offending groups who once provided easy punch lines, and tossed out cringe-inducing stereotypes—the swishy gay; jive-talking African Americans; Asians with thick accents. From where I sit, this is all fine and good, but as certain comedic tropes were left to the dustbin of comedic history, other tired stereotypes were shoved center stage to pick up the slack—in particular, the big, dumb, lazy, bumbling, hapless, ever-suffering dad.

The Cheerios Dad, the punk-rock dads of *The Other F Word*, Duff McKagan—across our culture, we're seeing men reject the tired image and showcase fatherhood in all its glory. If the creators of our fiction are slow to showcase characters who are role models of fatherhood, we who live in the world of nonfiction will just showcase them ourselves. No need for a Million Dad March, or an act of Congress, or bumbling-dad trigger words…we're too busy for all that sort of thing anyway.

We're dads. We're getting it done. Our wives, kids, friends, and neighbors should expect nothing less.

What Would Ward Cleaver Do?

He never pursued a life of excess from which he had to repent; he was wiser than that—and when it comes down to it, more manly, welcoming the heavy lifting, and extreme rewards, that come with responsibility, marriage, and kids.

---

* "Dad Life (Father's Day Opening 2010)," YouTube, https://www.youtube.com/watch?v=DOKuSQIJlog.

23

Settling Down Isn't Settling for Less

 It seems to be a given that getting married and having kids, particularly in your twenties, means that you're missing out on something. Why on earth would you want to start a family when you could do fabulously single and childless things?

Matt and Jessica Johnson, formerly of Grand Rapids, Michigan, may be the poster couple for a life free of responsibility. The pair, now in their early thirties, have been sailing around the world since 2011 in a sailboat that they purchased after they quit their jobs and sold off almost all of their belongings. Since then they've lived frugally and have traveled to sixteen different countries. They don't have any kids, but they did adopt a cat in 2012, so there's that.

Quitting your job as a car salesman or a billing specialist in Grand Rapids and heading for the warm waters of the Caribbean sounds awesome, but there are lots of things to consider before plunging into your new life. Can you really downsize your entire life to fit into a sailboat?

Can you spend twenty-four hours a day up close and personal with your partner? How do you decide who's The Skipper and who's Gilligan?

Not to mention the fact that selling all your stuff and living off of the savings means that at some point your money is likely to run out. It's one thing for our government to rack up insane and unimaginable amounts of debt, but you're not going to be able to do the same. When the money runs out, you're going to have to figure out what happens next. Maybe you sell the boat and start over? Maybe you settle down in a beach town and find another job? Based on their website, MJSailing.com, the Johnsons seem like really nice people who are having a great time. I hope they have many years of happiness ahead of them, wherever their sailboat may take them, but I also hope they have an exit strategy.

I also understand the impulse, as Matt Johnson described it, of wanting to live your dream while you can and not put it off until retirement. I remember having similar conversations with my wife: we talked often about moving from the suburbs to a farm "one day," without doing much to make it happen.

In that respect, you have to applaud the couple for actually turning their goal into a reality. Most people reading their story on their website will likely feel a little envious. Some folks might even think to themselves, "I'm gonna do that too!" Most of them won't get any further than looking at sailboats online. They'll dream about another life instead of making tangible improvements to the life they have now.

Most Americans in their twenties still want a life that includes marriage and family, according to virtually every survey out there. And yet, fewer of them are getting married, and even fewer are having kids. Some might fear the financial commitment; others the personal commitment. And some are no doubt delaying marriage and family because settling down feels like settling for less than the life you have as a single person.

But "settling down" is actually the biggest freaking adventure you could ever possibly undertake. You want to explore the unknown and push yourself further than you think possible? Get married. Maybe you want to see life in all its Technicolor glory, instead of the drab grays of the cubicle farm where you work. Have a child and you'll start seeing the world through their eyes. *Everything* will be new to you again.

There is no One True Dad Life to be lived. Being a stay-at-home dad is great if you can do it, but some of the best fathers I know are guys who spent months away from home on multiple deployments to Iraq, Afghanistan, and places they're not allowed to talk about. We have a lot of truck drivers who listen to NRA News' *Cam & Co* every night (I call them our Road Warriors), and I know many of them are gone from their homes for weeks at a time. When they're at home, though, they're *present*. They're involved in lives beyond their own.

I have some personal experience with this. When my wife and I decided to move from the suburbs of Washington, D.C., to central Virginia, my job didn't move with us. We knew when we moved that I would still be working near D.C., which was about three hours away from the home we'd found. There was no way to commute daily. Instead I would have to drive home on the weekends and the rare weekday evening. For a year and a half that's what I did, renting a 10x10 spare bedroom in a private home not too far from work. I'd drive the 150 or so miles home each Friday night, arriving around 10 p.m. We'd have all weekend to spend together, but every Monday morning after dropping the kids off at school I'd make the long drive back to northern Virginia. Every couple of weeks I'd come home on a Wednesday night, just to see my wife, sleep in my bed, and hang out with the kids for an hour in the morning. It was hard, but that time period also had a lot of great moments, and every one of them took place in those hours I spent with my family.

Consumer culture, technology, and social media have offered us an ever broadening array of "choice" in our lives, but they've also narrowed us as people, nurturing a culture of instant gratification and pervasive narcissism. The late writer David Foster Wallace warned us, in his 2005 commencement speech at Kenyon College, to be careful that we don't simply indulge what he called the "freedom all to be lords of our tiny skull-sized kingdoms, alone at the center of all creation."

The truly important freedom, the one that is most precious, Wallace said, "involves attention and awareness and discipline, and being able truly to care about other people and to sacrifice for them over and over again in myriad, petty, unsexy ways every day."

That sounds like a pretty good definition of being a spouse and a parent, in my opinion. Caring about others and sacrificing for them means taking on responsibility, but it also means freedom from a mindless shuffle through life. Given that he was speaking at a college commencement, perhaps it's not surprising that David Foster Wallace expounded on how education can be an escape hatch to the mindful life, but so is marriage and family. The trick is—whether it's reading great books, building a great marriage, or raising great kids—putting in the effort. Nothing happens by itself.

Granted, it's not easy. It's heavy lifting. And when we're not mindful, we can just go through the motions: get up, go to work, go home, watch TV, surf the Internet, go to bed, and then wake up and do it again. We're all human. But a family is a constant reminder to get out of your rut and engage with the people around you.

Family life, mindfully led, is guaranteed to be rich with adventure, wonder, and infinite opportunities to better yourself, your kids, and the world around you. No, you won't be able to avoid every hardship or tough time, but so what? Being a husband and father won't always be easy, but life isn't easy. At least when you're living the Dad Life, you don't have to do all the heavy lifting alone.

Get out there. Don't be afraid. Sure, have fun. Backpack through Belize. Live in a yurt for a couple of years. Float on a boat if that's what...er, floats your boat. But don't close your mind to getting married and making lots of babies. Fatherhood isn't boring, it's actually pretty badass. The only way that family life is boring is if you make it that way. Settling down with a wife and kids that you love isn't settling for less. In fact, it could be more than you ever thought possible.

What Would Ward Cleaver Do?

You know the answer to that. And Ward Cleaver was a stud.

Acknowledgments

 For quite a few months, my life featured the unnerving irony of declaring, "sorry, boys, Daddy can't play with you now. I have to finish my book on the importance of fatherhood." The boys and my wife are spectacularly patient with me, and I doubt I'll ever thank them enough.

Cam, I've known since our first talks in 2004 that you had many, many books within you, just waiting to be written. I'm honored to be your copilot on this one.

To all my friends who made cameo appearances in these pages...thank you for everything over all these years. These tales are supposed to show off my flubs and foibles, not yours.

A day job of writing at *National Review* is just about the best a writer can hope for; thanks to Rich Lowry, Jack Fowler, and everyone else at NR for their support and camaraderie.

 It would have been impossible for me to have contributed to this book without the support of my family. My wife and kids were patient and understanding during the weekends and evenings that I spent writing, and I am forever grateful for their love and support.

Thanks as well to all my family, friends, and professional associates who've lent their ears, expertise, and insight throughout the writing process. Your time, energy, and friendship are greatly appreciated.

Thanks also to my colleagues at NRA News for making it possible for me to take on a book project in addition to my job as host of NRA News' *Cam & Co.* I couldn't have done this without you, and I'm lucky to work with so many outstanding individuals.

A huge debt of gratitude is owed to the many individuals who have inspired me to be a better husband, father, and man. In particular, the members of our military who deploy overseas and the families they leave behind that I have known have given me a much greater appreciation of how precious family time can be. I've been honored to get to know the guys behind the Duskin & Stephens Foundation, named for fallen warriors Mike Duskin and Riley Stephens. These guys were badass warriors, but they were also family men, and the mission of the foundation is to support the families of fallen Special Ops warriors and the educational needs of the children of active duty Special Operation Forces. These warriors and their families do some real heavy lifting on behalf of all of us.

I have to thank my friend Jim Geraghty for asking me to write this book with him. We've been friends for a long time, and I wasn't particularly worried about our friendship being affected by the process of writing a book together. In retrospect, that was pretty foolish of me. I don't think you can do something like this in collaboration with a friend without it impacting your relationship. In this case, luckily enough, our friendship actually grew as the project came together. Thanks for everything, Jim.

 Our team at Regnery has been just the right blend of enthusiasm and veteran professionalism. Thank you Marji Ross, Harry Crocker, Maria Ruhl, and the rest of the gang. We also want to thank our agent, Mel Berger, for handling all the little details with the fine-tuned skill that is all too easy to take for granted.

Index

G

S